The Sanative Rose

Braijene Fletcher

ISBN 978-1-63821-306-2

Printed in USA by 48HrBooks (www.48HrBooks.com)

Dedication

My name is Braijene Fletcher, and this book is dedicated to diabetics around the world. I want you to know that even though you have diabetes, do not let that identify who you are. We are some of the strongest people in this world and you must remember that. Don't set limitations for yourself. Even on the days when you're awake at night; too dizzy to get out of bed treating a low blood sugar, when you're super-heated from a high blood sugar, when you're craving something sweet, and you eat it but regret it later…you will be okay. God is watching over you and I am praying for you.

Foreword

Braijene Fletcher is an aspiring, author who uniquely depicts her passion and love for others to win in life. "The Sanative Rose" shows her true character is of love, friendship, understanding, and compassion but most of all, faith. These are modeled as keys to victory and tools to success in the book. She has taken the struggles and hopes of sickness from real life to the pages of this dynamic book. She encourages the potential and power in the youth to not only survive but overcome even incurable diseases. This book will make a profound awareness of juvenile diabetes, as well as other health challenges and their needs. It will make a forever impact and influence in the lives of many as it has for me personally.

Pastor Dr. Carol Caldwell

Acknowledgement

First off, I would like to thank God for using me as a vessel to create this book. Without Him, this story would not have been made.

I would like to thank Mr. Chico, for taking the time to edit this book; as well as give feedback. I am a better writer because of you, and you are one of my favorite teachers.

To my First Lady Carol Caldwell of First Baptist World Changers International Ministries, thank you for being a guidance as far as helping me know why I am writing this book. All the phone calls we had reading scriptures; strengthening my faith, meant a lot to me.

To my family, Mom, Brielle, Bailey, and Balice, thank you for listening to me go on and on about my stories. With you guys by my side, I couldn't have asked for anything else. Balice...thank you for encouraging me.

And once again, thank you God for creating this story that's going to help so many people. You are the only reason I am alive today, Father, and I will continue to praise you, now and forever. I love you.

Table of Contents

Chapter 1 The Party 7

Chapter 2 The Club.......................... 22

Chapter 3 School............................. 42

Chapter 4 Friday.............................. 69

Chapter 5 The Date.......................... 88

Chapter 6 Diabetes 103

Chapter 7 Sunday 129

Chapter 8 The Carnival 140

Chapter 9 Friendship 165

Chapter 10 Homecoming 185

Chapter 11 The Hospital 197

Chapter 12 The Funeral 212

Chapter 13 MJ............................... 229

Chapter 14 New Beginnings........ 234

Bible Scriptures 257

His Closure................................... 260

Chapter One The Party

"This is the confidence we have in approaching God: that if we ask anything according to his will, he hears us."
1 John 5:14.

I look around for my purse, trying to figure out where I put it.

"COME ON, BRAY. WE'RE GOING TO BE LATE FOR THE PARTY."

Dang, why do I always have to be late for everything? I think to myself, shaking my head.

I mean, I'm late for school almost every single day.

"I CAN'T FIND MY PURSE, I HAVE NO IDEA WHERE I PUT IT."

"DID YOU CHECK THE DRAWER?"

Drawer?

I walk over to my dresser, finding my purse in it, feeling stupid of how I placed it there in the first place. Something's wrong with me…?

I laugh to myself. "FOUND IT."

"THEN COME ON."

I walk over to the bedroom door and I look at myself in the mirror that hangs on the wall behind it. This guest bedroom is where I stay whenever I spend the night over my big sister's house. 1 bedroom downstairs and 3 bedrooms on the 2nd floor. I personally find this house intimidating. There's been many times a tree branch has knocked on the window while I was sleeping. It scares the mess out of me. She stays in this house by herself but when my family and I want to spend time with her, there's enough space.

My brown skin is glistening in the half-dark room from the lotion I put on. My long, shaped nails, painted in a red shade, matching with my red crop top and a black jean jacket with red roses on it. My hair is curled in perfect shape with a side part as some of my bangs touch my forehead. My full lips covered with a faint, red gloss. My lashes are enhanced from mascara and my eyebrows are arched perfectly. My black, jean skirt and black wedges match perfectly. I smile, looking at my appearance.

My first high school party. I think to myself, shaking my head in amusement. "...Please let everything go okay Jesus...I pray that something good will happen. Amen."

I always wanted to go to a high school party. I hope I'm not overdressed.

"BRAY, IF YOU DON'T COME DOWN HERE RIGHT NOW, I'M GOING TO BED."

"OKAY OKAY, I'M COMING."

I walk out of my room and into the hallway that leads to the curved stairs. Brii is waiting at the end.

Her hair is pushed up in a curly bun and is wearing a Pink outfit. She loves Victoria's Secret.

I reach the end of the stairs and she gives me an annoyed look. "Where was it?"

"In the drawer," I shrug.

8

"You've been coming over here for a whole three years and you still don't remember where to put things."

"Your house is…"

She raises her eyebrow.

"What?"

"Never mind, it's fine."

She presses. "What?"

"Nothing."

"Hmm okay. Anyways you look pretty Bray. I like the floral pattern." she grins at me.

"Thank you, you do too and I'm wearing my jacket just in case it gets cold…and tell Myrah thanks again for curling my hair," I look down at myself. I start sashaying around with a smirk on my face and she rolls her eyes while cracking a smile.

"Told you she can curl pixies. Are you sure you'll be able to walk in those heels?

"Of course, I walk better than you in heels," I laugh.

"Shut up," she walks towards the door.

I really do walk better in heels than Brii does. I remember a time where Brii was in a pageant. Mom bought her these 5-inch heels and I had to give her lessons on how to walk in them.

I smile to myself. "I'll bring my flats if you put them in your purse,"

"Duh," she says.

I grab my black flats off the floor that sits by her gigantic door and put them in Brii's purse. "Did you grab your insulin?" Brii asks.

"Right."

I scurry to the dining room that leads to the kitchen. I head towards the freezer to grab my freezer bag and open the refrigerator side to take my insulin out. Putting my insulin -both Apidra and Lantus- and needles into the bag, I check to make sure I have all my supplies before grabbing my purse off the table and following Brii outside to her car.

"So, are you excited for your first high school party?" she smiles.

"Yeah, I am but I'm a little nervous."

"Why?"

I hunch my shoulders before saying, "I guess 'cause I don't know what's going to happen." I look out the window.

"I'm gonna be there to make sure nothing happens to you," she playfully pushes me. "And to make sure you check your blood sugar."

I playfully roll my eyes. "Okay."

"What's the girl's name that invited you?"

"Her name's Ashley. She's in the 10th. I have a speech class with her."

My 7th period is the only class I have that includes upperclassmen.

"Okay," she says and turns up the radio.

For the rest of the drive, we listen to music and talk. I enjoy car rides with my big sister. She's improved so much as a driver and there's never a conversation, I don't enjoy with her. Even though, she sometimes can be a bit judgy and mean, I love her either way. After almost an hour, we finally arrive at the party. Getting out of the car, I scan the house.

Not as big as I thought it would've been…it's actually small.

As we walked through the side of the house, there was an altar over the gate, which led to the backyard.

"This altar is so pretty," I say.

Taking a few more steps, I was amazed at how big Ashley's backyard was.

Oh my gosh.

I stop and take everything in.

Oval-shaped pool, a stage with a D.J, a dance floor…

Dang, that's a long table.

I don't think I've ever seen a table with so much food, desserts, and drinks.

"Dang, this party lit," says Brii.

I look at her in agreement.

"Hey, Bray,"

I hear someone call my name, snapping me out of my thoughts. I turn around and see Ashley walking towards me.

Her 4c hair is in a puffball, edges swooped, and she is wearing a dark green jumper. The lights hanging around compliment her brown skin.

"Thanks for coming. Enjoy the party," she hugs me.

I hug her back and say, "Thanks, Ashley. This is my big sister Brii." I gesture towards her.

"Hi, nice to meet you," she smiles at Brii.

"Hi, you too."

"Help yourself to anything you like. There's more than enough." she walks off.

"Let's go get a drink," I say.

"Okay."

We walk to the very end of the long table. I look at each punch bowl and read the label.

Alcoholic Drinks. I get slightly irritated. *Of course, there'd be alcohol.*

I look over to see a sign that says 'Non-Alcoholic Drinks' Brii picks up two cups and pours herself and I some pop.

I take a sip and turn myself toward the dance floor.

"You gonna go dance?" Brii takes a sip of her pop.

"Nah, probably not."

"Why not? Go show everyone what you got."

"Only if you come with me," I give her a fake smile as I start to get nervous.

Should I? I don't know...maybe... I sometimes get nervous if I have to dance under these circumstances.

"Now you know I can't dance. You better go dance for real though, or I'm leaving you," she gives me a dumb look.

"Okay fine! Dang, we just got here and you're already acting like that." I roll my eyes at her. She sighs, rolls her eyes, and looks at me.

I look around. "But only when a song I know comes on,"

"Okay."

As I stood there talking with Brii, I noticed a few boys were staring and smirking at her.

Gosh, I wish I turned heads as she does. She's so pretty.

Her light skin, almost yellow complexion match perfectly with her light brown eyes and light brown hair. Even though I jokingly call her 'chubby', she is very thick…in the right places. My 'fat cheeks'.

I mentally laugh at the nickname I gave Brii.

"Aye Brii, you got some fans staring at you," I gesture their way.

She looks and hunches her shoulders. That's when the song 'Cabin in Manolo' comes on by Trip Lee. So I give Brii my cup and run to the dance floor.

"Good thing you put those flats on, crazy," she calls out to me and I smile.

I start dancing and see a bunch of people circling me. They're taking pictures and videotaping. At some points, I catch a glimpse of Brii with her phone out taping also. Other people join in with me as we dance the same moves. Soon, the song starts going out, and everyone comes in the middle- squishing me, starting to jump up and down. I finally manage to get out of the crowd and go to get some water. I look around for Brii but can't find her. I sigh in frustration as I spot my wedges in front of the table.

"Nice going Brii." I roll my eyes.

I change into them and put my flats into my purse.

"Wow." I hear a deep voice behind me.

I turn my head to see a boy with brown skin; just slightly lighter than mine, and shaped curly hair; pouring himself some pop.

"You must be a really dedicated dancer if you thought to bring two pairs of shoes." he takes a sip of his drink and puts one hand inside his loose pant's pocket.

13

Woah, he's handsome and his voice...that's attractive. His voice is attractive. How can a voice be attractive?

"Hey, I came prepared," I smile. "One pair for the dance floor and the other...to make me look taller." he chuckles showing his perfect set of teeth and I giggle with him.

Gulping down the rest of his drink, he sets it down on the table and walks over to me. As his eyes never leave mine, I can feel my heartbeat quicken as he gets closer and closer. As he is walking, I realize just how tall he is. Even with the heels on, I still have to look up at him.

"You are pretty short. How tall are you?" he asks with a smile on his face.

"5'1," I say. "And a half...and you?" I ask.

"5'10...and a half."

We continue to look at each other as awkward tension forms.

Okay...

"Well...guess the heels aren't working."

He scratches the back of his head and chuckles as I look down and giggle. This is kind of funny how we don't know what to say.

I hope he knows how to carry a conversation.

"I'm Trey." he holds his hand out.

I take his hand. "Bray."

He shakes my hand and I get a nervous feeling in my stomach. As we stand there, I decide to take in his features.

He has a perfectly structured face with a jawline that could cut fruit, full lips, and medium-sized eyes...his eyes.

My attraction to him is growing even more just looking at them. His eyes look brown and green but I'm sure they're brown with a touch of green because we're not in the sunlight. I can feel the tension grow more as he continues to hold onto my hand. I slowly let go and awkwardly look around.

I really hope he can't tell how nervous I am. I have no problem talking to people I don't know. In this case, this gorgeous guy who approached me. It's just, when I find the guy attractive, I tend to get a little tongue-tied.

Oh God, give me the confidence I need, Lord!

"Um-

"But anyway, you're a good dancer," he smirks.

"Thanks," I say.

"Are you serious about dancing? How long have you been dancing?" he asks.

"Yeah...and ever since I was 6."

"Really..."

I nod.

"I've been one since I was 9. Hip Hop mostly, but I can do a few tricks in jazz," he says.

"That's cool," I smile. "Are you with a particular program?"

"I was once, for two years when I was younger...things happened and I had to get out of it," he hunches his shoulders.

"Which program was it?"

"Riverside Dance Factory."

15

"Really? Well, I'm with the 'Wayne County Dance Program.'" I say, doing a little twirl.

"The arch-nemesis I see," he smirks.

I laugh.

"Yeppers." I say.

"Riverside is better," he says while rubbing his hands together.

I scoff. "Uh, excuse me?"

He turns to look at me.

"Wayne Dance Program is better, and won 1st place, seven times this year."

"Okay but Riverside has won just as many times…even if it wasn't this year."

"Wayne's still better."

"Maybe we'll settle it on the dance floor one day."

I scrunch my eyes. "I just might take you up on that."

"Alright bet."

"Okay." I smile and shake my head.

This conversation is…good.

"So, are you a Freshman, Sophomore-

"Freshman."

"…You look about 16, 17," he gives me an uncertain look.

I hunch my shoulders. "I get that a lot."

"How are you liking Westbrook?" he asks.

"It's good so far. I'm with my best friend so it's not like I'm alone…It's such a big school, I'm still trying to get used to that."

"Yeah, I understand."

"So what are you? Freshman, Junior, Sophomore-

"Freshman," he says.

"Now YOU don't look like it," I say, shocked.

"I get that a lot," he side-eyes me, giving me a smile.

"Actually, you look familiar," I say, thinking.

"Yeah, we have 7th hour together."

"Really?" I ask, feeling stupid for not realizing it before.

He nods slowly.

Two weeks have gone by, and I haven't noticed this boy...what is going on here?

I change the subject. "You enjoyin' the party?"

"Yeah, it's straight. To be honest, unless it's a dance event...parties like these, I'll make the exception to go if someone wants me to. Other than that, I'd rather be at home."

"Mmm...okay...doing what?"

"Probably watching Po-

"Okay!" I stop him and put my hand up.

He laughs, "I'm joking. If I'm being honest, I'd be reading, playing my instruments, or watching Pimple Popper."

I give him a shocked and disgusted look before stopping and putting both hands on my hair.

"Nope," I say, and he laughs.

I turn and walk away -not going too far- still shaking my head.

"Don't walk away." he chuckles, walking over to me.

"How can you watch that?" I make another disgusted look. "My sister watches that."

"It's satisfying."

I sigh. "No, it's disgusting."

I shake my head at him and twitch as I walk back to where we were before. He follows and looks at me, but I can't make out what he's thinking.

"So what about you? Are you a party person?" he asks.

"Yeah, I don't mind going as long as someone is with me. I don't know if I'll go by myself." I smile and shake my head in disbelief, "I'm actually here with my older sister, who I can't seem to find." I look around.

"I think you'll do just fine coming by yourself. You'll catch people's attention as soon as you walk in." he gazes down at me before winking.

I smile slightly and look away.

"You think your girlfriend would be cool with you flirting with me?" I look back at him.

"Girlfriend?" he remarks, with an uncertain look on his face.

"Yeah."

He locks eyes with me. "Nah, I don't have a girlfriend, baby girl."

Wow...that's a shocker there. This boy is literally one of the most handsome boys I've ever seen.

I lower my eyes and say, "I'm sorry for assuming."

"You good. Are you in any clubs?" he takes a few steps forward.

I follow and say, "Not yet but I want to audition for the drama club."

A boy runs past Trey and me and I roll my eyes as he almost hits me. I look at Trey as he is glaring at the boy. The boy looks back and apologizes.

"...Anyway, that's wassup. So, do you know what days you'd have to go?"

"Mondays and Wednesdays I think."

"So you're free Friday afternoons and Saturdays?"

"Yeah, Fridays but Saturdays I'm in this group thing from 12-2 pm. Why do you wanna know?"

"Um..." he puts his hands in his pockets, "I'd like to take you out."

I look at him confused with a smile on my face and then try to hide my smile.

Do I hide my smile? Should I keep a little grin?

"Really?"

"Yeah. What do you think?" he grins.

"I'll think about it and let you know."

"Okay...Can I get your number?

"Uh I actually don't give out my number, but you can have my Snapchat."

"Okay." he smiles.

We add each other on Snapchat, and I turn my head as I hear someone call Trey's name. I look back up at Trey as he looks down at me.

"Imma text you tomorrow...it was nice talking to you Bray,"

"You too, see you Monday"

"Alright baby girl."

He leaves and I smile to myself. Suddenly, I feel an arm on me. I jump and curse out, turning around.

"What the he-heck Brii?!"

She smiles. "I saw you talking to that boy,"

"Well, that's not stalker-ish at all," I shake my head before shrugging.

"He was cute."

"I know…he wants to take me out."

"What did you say?"

"I told him I'll think about it…I just met him."

"Right."

"I have a class with him, and I gave him my Snap…he was pretty cool," I look at Brii.

"Alright, just don't be telling everybody he tryin' to 'talk' to you. You already remember what happened with Tyler."

I look at her and then lower my head trying to forget what happened with an old friend.

"I know…now can we please enjoy the party."

"Yeah," she laughs.

Eventually, Brii and I decide to leave once it gets later in the evening. We danced together and ate some food. I checked my blood sugar each time Brii told me to, and while almost at the entrance to leave, I hear someone call my name.

"Heyyy Brayy," MJ says all hyper.

"Uh, hey…what are you doing here?" I say, concerned. "I thought your blood sugar was really high."

She'd never do anything like this, especially after she's just getting out of the hospital…something's wrong. Now I'm frustrated.

"MJ," I say,

"What? I'm just here to exercise, see, I got my dance suit on." MJ smiles.

I look at her black leggings and red, half shirt with black flowers on it. Her kinky, light brown hair is swooped into a perfect bun. Her red lip matches with her light-brown skin and even though she's wearing glasses, her eyes are glossy.

Her blood sugar must be really high...is she trying to match with me?

I give her a blank stare. "You can't dance."

A song she knows comes on and she curses while doing a funny dance to it.

"Pull up drop-top with a eater...two-seater."

I laugh and regain my seriousness.

"Let's take you home-

She playfully rolls her eyes. "No, can I at least stay for an hour MOM?"

I glare at her. "For real though, I don't want anything to happen to you," I say.

She pouts. "Nothing's going to happen. Come on, just stay with me for a bit...please"

"Fine, I'll stay but only for an hour, 'cause Brii is tired and so am I."

"Oh, hey Brii...didn't see you there."

Brii playfully rolls her eyes. "Hey, boo."

"Alright people, let's get this party started, now that MJ is here."

She pulls me with her to the dance floor and I start laughing.

Chapter Two The Cub
09/16

"Two is better than one because they have a good return for their labor. If either of them falls down, one can help the other up."
Ecclesiastes 4:9-10.

Saturday afternoon…

Brii and I are on our way to Lakeside hospital. The biggest hospital in Detroit and it's where I went when I was first diagnosed with my illness. I love the 15-minute drives to Lakeside. The scenery calms me. I've gotten used to living on this side of Detroit. We used to stay in Mexican town. Those were some pretty fun years…but it was time to move on so now we stay downtown and the only time we go to Mexican town is when we want food…and when we want to visit our friends…and when we want to shop. I mentally laugh to myself.

I rest my head on the window. "Thanks for going to the party with me Brii…I had fun."

"No problem, what time is it?"

"11:50," I say.

"Okay, we're almost here."

A few minutes later, we arrive at Lakeside Hospital.

She stops her car. "Alright…mom is picking you up, right?

"Yeah," I say.

She waves. "Okay have fun, love you."

"Love you too, bye."

She pulls off and I go inside. I walk through the huge room that leads to different directions. I make eye contact with Nurse Walker while she walks past the front desk.

"Hey, Nurse Walker."

She smiles. "Hey Bray."

I keep walking forward as a couple more nurses are walking in my direction.

I give them a big smile. "Hi, Nurse Raven and Nurse Nate,"

"Hi Bray." she smiles. "Sup, Bray." he gives me a high five.

"Is Nurse Patricia here?" I call out.

"She's working later on," Nate says.

"Awe, okay."

"Yeah. See you soon,"

"Bye."

Nurse Nate, Raven and Patricia are all the nurses who took care of me when I was first diagnosed with my illness. I appreciate them so much.

As I continue to walk down the hall, I hear heavy footsteps near me. I turn my head just as MJ hugs me. I almost stumble over but a slight smile is on my face.

"Hey, Bray,"

I hug her back. "Hey, girl,"

She must've been running.

"You enjoyed your first high school house party?" she asks.

"Yes, I did, thanks for asking," Sarcasm is clear in my voice. "Did you?"

"Heck yes."

I look at her with annoyance and she looks down.

After a few seconds, she says, "I wanted to apologize...I know I shouldn't have gone out last night...I'm sorry,"

"Don't apologize to me...apologize to yourself,"

She looks away from me.

I ask, "Where was your mom anyway?"

"Work. She had a night shift."

We arrive at the elevator and get in. She presses the 6th floor and I lean on the wall.

"So you snuck out?"

She fixes her glasses. "Not technically."

I look at her confused.

"My brother offered to take me," she looks at me.

"Your brother's a douchebag. He doesn't even care that you're just getting out of the hospital," I say, getting frustrated.

She hunches her shoulders. "Don't think he knew. It happens so often that it's just old news to him," she rolls her eyes.

I shake my head, praying things would be different for her. Because of MJ's blood sugar being high all the time, she comes to the hospital just about every 2 weeks. I'm not really sure why her sugar is always high, it just is. She takes her insulin, counts her carbs, but for some reason, it remains high...but when it goes super high, it causes her to not be able to breathe, so to the hospital she goes! I just hate the fact that she thought it was a good idea to come to the party last night when she just got out of the hospital a few hours earlier.

I look at her and she looks up, closing her eyes, looking like she's in deep thought. I try to read her but can't seem to figure it out.

After getting off the elevator, we finally get up to the room where some of our friends and Nurse Walker are at. We both read the scripture that is typed on a paper next to the door.

Luke 6:19 And the people all tried to touch Him, because power was coming from Him and healing them all.

I smile and we walk in.

"Good afternoon, guys, both of you look beautiful as always."

MJ and I speak together. "Why thank you."

We both laugh and say hi to everyone and take a seat. This room...I've grown so fond of. I've been coming here every Saturday for the last 3 years. I've made so many memories with this group. They are my family. The pictures hanging on our picture wall, the refrigerator and freezer in the front of the room, the decorations hanging around that represent our different backgrounds, and every encouraging quote and scripture on the wall makes this room my 3rd home...my 2nd home is The Custard Company...gotta love ice cream.

"Hey, guys."

"Hey, Rachelle," MJ says.

"Bello," I smile. "Love your outfit today."

"Ha, really?"

"Of course. The baggy look and the messy ponytail are always my go-to…that is if my hair was as long as yours." I playfully pout.

"Honestly it has been a lot recently. I told the doctors I wanted it pressed instead of wearing it natural."

"I bet it's at your lower back," MJ says.

Rachelle laughs. "It is."

I smile.

"That's right girl, dark skin girls can have hair too." MJ snaps her fingers.

We all laugh.

"What have you been up to this week?" I ask Rachelle.

"Same old, same old." she says, "What about you?"

"Second week of high school just passed, and MJ and I went to a party Friday," I give her a half-smile.

"Oh, did you have fun?"

"Yeah,"

"I'm glad for you."

"Thanks, Rache."

"Hey guys, I think we're getting a new member to the club," MJ says.

Rachelle asks, "How do you know?"

"Look."

The three of us look towards the door. There's a girl with a light complexion and blonde, brownish shoulder-length hair, with blue eyes and an oxygen tank with her.

"...She looks like that one girl," I say.

Rachelle and MJ look at me.

"What?"

"Everyone looks like 'that one girl' to you, Bray."

26

"Not true."

Nurse Belsh walks in. "Okay everyone, can I have your attention please?" we all look at her. "We have a new member to the club...everyone welcome, Mary-Kate."

"Hey."

"Hi."

"Sup"

"Now for today we're going to each take turns to say our name and age and why we're in the National Illness Club so Mary-Kate can get to know you guys more. You can also say an interesting fact...MJ, would you like to start?"

"Sure...Hey, my name is MJ Reeds. I'm 14 and I'm a type 1 diabetic. I've been a diabetic since I was 5. So...yeah. Oh, and I'm mixed with black and white."

"Hi, I'm Rachelle Johnson. I'm 15 years old. I have vitiligo as you can see, and I also have E.O.E. Eosinophilic esophagitis. That basically means that my esophagus and stomach are inflamed and swollen, and because of that, there's certain food I have to stay away from, and by certain, I mean a lot. Certain food gives me an allergic reaction so I can't eat like I used to. I've had the E.O.E for a year now. I've lost a lot of weight." she looks down. "But I have my best friends here to support me," she gestures towards MJ and me. We both smile and hold hands for a quick second. "I know I'm gonna get better soon and I also mostly live in the hospital too, so I don't get out much. My dad is Jamaican, and mom is from here."

"Hey Mary-Kate, I'm Bray Fletcher. I'm 14 and I'm also a type 1 diabetic. I've been a diabetic for three years now. The doctors can't even explain how I got it. It didn't come from my family though and I'm fully black." I grin.

"Wassup, I'm Ty Jones and I'm Kayla Jones...and we're twins."

They need to tell me about their skin routine. Their caramel skin is always glowing.

Ty stands up; his fit body is even more visible.

"We're 16 and we both have leukemia," says Ty.

Kayla, standing beside him as the height difference is clear says, "We've had it since childhood,"

Their unique blue eyes and brown, curly hair are so pretty.

"It's a type of cancer," Ty says.

"And we're Dominican and Black." Kayla states.

Ty laughs. "Why is everyone stating their race or ethnicity?"

"Like I'm trying to figure that out myself."

"I don't know. It kind of stuck after MJ said hers."

"My bad." MJ laughs.

We all giggle. Ty and Kayla sit back down and my eyes move to Kevin.

"...Hey, I'm Kevin Brooks."

His blonde and brown hair is messy and his usually tanned skin is a bit pale today.

"And I'm 15. I have thyroid cancer. My type is Medullary. I lost half of my left leg when I was 13 and I might be losing half my arm, unfortunately...and I'm white."

He turns his head to Chanel, waiting for her to speak.

She shows her perfect teeth. "I'm Chanel Trevino."

Chanel's olive skin is glistening in the sun from her sitting by the window. Her usually straight, dark-brown hair is curled in loose waves.

"And I'm 16. I have pseudotumor cerebri. Meaning that there's a ton of pressure around my brain, causing me to have blurred vision and headaches, and a few other things. I am also bipolar. And…I'm Mexican and Italian.

"Hey, I'm Cory Randold."

Corey's words are muffled as he is drowning in his huge hoodie.

"Corey, do you think you can take the hood off just for a quick second?" Nurse Walker asks.

He sighs and takes his hood off. I smile as I notice his now new buzz cut hair. He looks up.

"What? I just didn't want you guys to see my hair."

"Looks good bro," Ty says to him and Corey smiles.

He then looks at Mary-Kate and repeats himself.

"I'm 16 and I have Crouzon Syndrome. I was born with it." he gestures to his face.

We all look at Mary-Kate.

"Well, hi everyone, as you all know I'm Mary-Kate Daniels and I have Thyroid Cancer." she looks at Kevin. "My type is Medullary too and I need more oxygen for my lungs, that's why I have this."

She gestures down to her oxygen tank.

"Nice to meet all of you guys too," she softly smiles. "And you can call me MK."

"Okay everyone, let's circle around. We're getting a new wristband with colors, light blue, and gold. So everyone, grab one and write your number down." says

29

Nurse Belsh. "And make sure you wear the wristband every time you come."

We each take one and sit at the table.

"I see you still have that broken phone. Why won't you just get it fixed Ty?" says MJ.

" 'Cause my parents want me to work for it. Keep saying I need to get a job," he says, sarcastically while rolling his eyes.

"Ha, with yo clumsy butt, you can't do jack," MJ says.

We all laugh.

Ty playfully pushes her over. "Yeah, thanks, MJ,"

MJ pushes him back. "Don't push me, big head,"

I laugh as they begin to 'play fight'. Then, Kevin comes and sits by me, sitting on the chair backward. He looks handsome.

He smiles. "How have you been doing Bray?"

"I'm pretty okay…how about you?"

"Not so great." I look at him confused. "The doctors found a tumor in my arm and if they don't get it out, I could lose half of it."

"Are you serious? They said nothing was there at your last check-up. Why are they saying this now?"

He hunches his shoulders. "They said they missed it by mistake. You know how doctors are these days…"

I shake my head.

I start to get teary-eyed. "I'm so sorry."

"Don't worry about it…I'm just going to pray and trust God. Remember, in Jesus Christ's stripes I am healed."

I smile at him and give him a long hug. He rubs my hair and back.

"You smell good," he pulls away and smiles.

I giggle and say, "Thanks, you do too, you weirdo."

"Um...who's the oldest between you two?" Mary-Kate asks Kayla.

"He is...by 3 minutes." she looks at her.

"So Mary-Kate, how old are you?" asks Rachelle.

"16," she says.

"What school you go to," MJ asks.

"Cranbrook High."

"Cool,"

"I heard they have a lot of cool clubs there. Are you in any?" I ask.

"Neh, I only wanted to be in this on Saturdays. It's nice to be around people that go through different things but same as you."

"Well, girl, you're gonna like it here. Just make sure you watch out for Ty. He farts a lot." MJ laughs.

Everyone laughs and Ty says, "You know what MJ? That is not true, don't listen to her, Mary-Kate."

"Now we all know MJ is no one to talk. You go around farting on people and scare them every time we're here." Corey says, disgustedly in a good way.

We all laugh so hard.

MJ folds her arms. "Hey, what can I say? I'm nice that way."

"MJ, you gotta stop with the scares for real though...I almost peed my pants the last time," Kayla says.

"Hahaha."

"And you filmed it, Bray, don't laugh. You're just as bad."

I laugh so hard I can barely breathe. "It was so funny," I finally say.

Chanel gets up and starts talking to Nurse Belsh.

"Wanna see Mary-Kate?"

"Sure."

I take out my phone and press Snapchat to show her the video. We both laugh as we watch MJ scare the rest of the members.

"You'll get used to all this. Trust me, you'll like it here," Kevin says to Mary-Kate.

She smiles.

Nurse Belsh stands in the middle of the room. "Did everyone read the 'scripture of the week' by the door?"

"Yeppers!"

"Yep."

"Yes."

After a few seconds, Nurse Belsh says, "Luke 6:19, And the people all tried to touch Him, because power was coming from Him and healing them all...like I've been teaching you guys, Jesus is our healer. No matter what illness you have, mental, physical, or even spiritual...the only one who can cure your diseases is Jesus. He may use different doctors and medicines to help, but it's always Him."

I smile as Nurse Belsh continues.

***

After the meeting is over, I say goodbye to everyone, and MJ and I walk to the main entrance with Kevin.

32

"Bray, I can still come over, right?" MJ asks.

"Yeah, my mom said it was cool."

"Good,"

"You know, we gotta talk to Nurse Belsh about our own National Illness Club (N.I.C.)," I say.

"I know, we will soon,"

Kevin asks, "You guys still want your own club?"

"Yeah, it's been our dream ever since I joined," I say.

MJ wants to be a nurse when she grows up. Once, I came into the club, we decided to start one together. Now that we're a little bit older, we finally can.

"Nurse Belsh said that once we get confirmation from the hospital, we can start ours with little kids on Saturdays too. We really want this," MJ says. "We want to help people with their illnesses. Help them cope with it."

We smile at each other. After a few more steps, we reach the entrance of the hospital. There are a lot more people in the waiting area.

"I think you guys are awesome for wanting to do that." Kevin says to us.

"Nurse Belsh is pretty awesome herself," I say.

"We all love her...well, I'll see you guys later," he gives me a big hug.

"Bye Kevin," I say.

"See you next week," MJ hugs him.

MJ and I walk outside and wait for my mom to pull up from the long line of cars in front of us.

MJ smiles at me. "Ya know, you and Kevin would look so cute together,"

"Girl, you know him and I are just friends."

"Yeah, but y'all would be a cute couple. He already likes you."

"I know, but we're just close friends."

"Mhm," she smirks.

"Speaking of couples…a boy at the party asked me out," I smile.

"Oh my gosh, who?"

"His name's Trey. He's a freshman."

"And when was this?"

"It was like three hours before you came, I think."

"Was he cute?"

"Yes, that boy was fine, okay?" I smile uncontrollably.

She does a little dance. "Oooh, Bray's boutta have herself a boyfriend,"

"We don't know that…you're so crazy…stop, people are looking."

She continues dancing and starts booty bumping me, making me laugh.

"Girl, come on, get down with me,"

I start dancing with her and we both laugh, "And anyway, I told him I'll think about it."

She stops dancing and says, "You're so lucky."

"What about you and Ty?" I tease her. "I know you have a crush on him,"

"Ugh. I know, but I don't think he likes me."

"Of course, he does. Just tell him. He might like you back. Wait, never mind, don't tell him. Let him say SOMETHING first."

"I don't know…here's your mom."

I spot my mom's car and she pull up in front of us before getting in.

I give her a hug. "Hey, Mom,"

"Hey, and hey MJ," she says.

"Hi, Ms. Fletcher."

"So how was it today?" my mom asks.

"It was good. We got a new member today."

"Oh?"

"Her name's Mary-Kate, and what disease does she have again?" I look back at MJ.

"It was Thyroid cancer, I think."

"Oh, okay," Mom says.

"She was pretty cool I guess."

"Yeah,"

Mom says to MJ, "So how have you been, giirrll,"

"I've been okay," MJ says.

"I tried calling your mom. She wasn't answering."

"Yeah, um, her phone broke. I don't know when she'll be getting it fixed."

"Okay, well who should I call to pick you up?"

"My brother," she says.

"Okay. You enjoyed the party yesterday, Bray?"

"Yeah, it was awesome. Brii and I had a great time."

"That's good. Do you guys want some Wendy's?"

"Oooh yes," I say.

"Yes please."

After going to Wendy's, it takes us another 10 minutes to arrive at my house. The green and white on the outside of my house is so aesthetically pleasing. 1 bedroom on the first floor and 4 on the 2nd. A nice, big kitchen, a huge living room, with the biggest backyard on the block. My room even has a balcony…I argued with my sisters over the room. I was determined to get it! We go inside and see my two younger, twin sisters watching T.V.

"Hey, you guys,"

They both speak together. "Hey Bray."

"Mom got some Wendy's, so here y'all go. Brii here?" I ask.

"Yeah, she's about to leave though," says Balice.

"Alright. Well, tell her I said hey."

"Okay," she says.

MJ walks to the couch. "Hey Bailey and Balice."

They both say. "Heyy,"

MJ goes and gives them a hug. We both head up to my room to watch a movie and eat our food. When the movie goes off, we get on FaceTime and talk to everyone in the club except for Mary-Kate.

"Hey, shouldn't we invite Mary-Kate?" I ask.

"Why not?" says Corey.

"None of us have her number," says Ty.

"I do." Chanel says, "Let me try to call her now…she didn't answer."

"Oh well, next time then," I say.

After an hour of being on FaceTime, Balice walks into my room.

She says, "Mom wants you to wash the dishes, Bray,"

"Okay."

"Sorry guys, gotta wash the dishes."

"Peace," says Ty.

"Bye y'all," says Kayla.

"Okay," Corey says.

"Alright see you Bray and MJ," Chanel says.

"Bye," says Kevin.

"Bye guys," Rachelle says.

I press the hang up button. MJ and I head downstairs into the kitchen. I wash the dishes and MJ dries them off. At times, I splash a little bit of water on her and she smacks me with the towel. As I finish washing the last dish, I notice her singing a song.

"I don't wanna be alive, I don't wanna be alive, I just wanna die today, I just wanna die."

She repeats it another time while drying the last dish. She sits down.

"Are you okay? You've been acting a little weird lately."

She glances up at me. "Weird how?"

"I don't know, but do you wanna talk about the party?"

"What about it?" she asks, confused.

"It's just, that's not something you would've done, ya know? I mean, you know how serious your diabetes is. You just got out of the hospital, and you came to a party with your sugar high, not feeling well."

"Look, I know it wasn't right but I was just upset that I couldn't go with you to the party and I know it's not a good excuse but you don't know how bad I wanted to come. So I had my brother take me and he didn't try to stop me," she looks at me with sincerity.

"You know I would've just blown it off, and we could've had a girl's night."

"I know, but I knew how much you wanted to go and your mom wasn't gonna let you unless Brii went. I didn't want you to miss it and I didn't either," she gives me a sad smile.

With a concerned look on my face, I ask, "Are you sure it's nothing else?"

"Yes, it's nothing else."

She hugs me.

"MJ, YOUR BROTHER IS HERE." my mom calls out.

"COMING."

I send MJ to get the door and I run upstairs to grab her purse. I come back down to find her brother at the door with her.

What is this boy wearing?

His dark brown shirt, blue jeans, and red cap reminds me of a character…ah, Lil Bill. I mentally laugh to myself.

He smirks at me. "Wassup cutie,"

MJ hits him on the side of his head.

"Shut up with your 19-year-old self," MJ says.

I roll my eyes and say, "Hey Lil Bill,"

He glares at me and I give her her purse.

"And next time don't offer to take her to a party knowing dang well she wasn't supposed to be doing anything, after just getting out of the hospital," I glare daggers at him.

"Well I don't care what you think and I will do anything I please babe,"

"Don't call me babe."

"Sorry, babe."

I say a few curse words and say goodbye to MJ. I shut the door.

He is one irritating person.

After making sure they left, I go into the kitchen to check my blood sugar. I grab my blood sugar kit and take out the meter, strips, and pricker. I put a strip into the meter and grab an alcohol pad to clean my finger. I prick my finger and squeeze a little bit of blood out and wipe that with the alcohol pad. I squeeze a bit more blood out and let the strip suck up the blood so the meter can calculate my blood sugar. I wait five seconds.

"180,"

Pretty good.

I take the strip out the meter and throw the alcohol pad and strip away. After everything is back in my pouch, I look into the refrigerator and grab my Lantus pin. I then grab a pin needle and take the top off and twist it onto the Lantus pin. I take the safety off the needle and turn the scale on the pin to "2" and press the bottom to let the air out. Then, I turn the scale to "20" and I take my shot in my thigh. I wait ten seconds before slowly pulling the needle out. After unscrewing the pin needle off the insulin pin, throwing it away, and putting the pin back in the refrigerator, I grab two kid-size crunch bars and pour myself ¼ cup of juice. I walk down the hall to go upstairs, and I say goodnight to everyone before going to my room. I take out my drawing book and finish a drawing I've been working on. After that, I grab my camera off my nightstand and look through some videos and pictures. I edit a few pictures and then take out my phone. I google different Illness clubs and colors to figure out what I like. I am more of a night owl, so I do a lot of things at night. As I drift off to sleep, I feel my phone vibrate. Tired, I pick it up to see a notification from Snapchat.

"Hey Bray?"

"who's this?"

"This Trey."

"Oh hey," I giggle at his username. "Thought you were gonna call me earlier."

"Yeah, I'm sorry about that, something came up."

"For the whole day?" I ask.

"You were waiting for me to call, weren't you?" He sends an emoji.

"No."

"Admit it, you were."

"In your dreams."

"Mhm. Okay, Bray. I "so" believe you."

"Whatever." I giggle to myself.

"How was your day?" he asks.

I let three minutes pass before replying again.

"Pretty good. How 'bout you?"

"I've had better."

"What happened?... if you don't mind me asking."

"Family issues. No big deal."

"I'm sorry to hear that."

"You good, not your fault...ya know I wasn't expecting you to be up."

"On Saturdays, I stay up late, but I was actually about to go to sleep lol."

"Oh, my bad baby girl...you were on my mind all day. I had to talk to you like I promised.

I smile to myself.

"Good to know," I say.

"Yeah...well if you're tired, we can talk tomorrow." he texts.

"Alright...goodnight."

"Sweet dreams baby girl."

"You too." I put my phone down and smile to myself.

I begin to pray.

"I pray MJ and I will be able to start our club, in Jesus name...Amen."

I snuggle myself into my covers and go to sleep.

Chapter Three School

"The pain that you've been feeling can't compare to
the joy that's coming."
Romans 8:18.

flashback

A year ago at Lakeside Hospital 1:05 p.m

Corey and I were looking for more supplies to
finish our art projects in the club. I was able to find some
more glue, so I put it in a bag on the floor. I was looking
under a few shelves until Corey called my name.
"Bray, Bray, come here!"
"What?" I asked, walking over to Corey.
"Mind telling me who this is?"
"What are you talking about?"
Corey held up my phone revealing a text from a boy
I know. It read 'hey beautiful'.
"No one. Just a friend."
He handed me my phone. "Mhm, just know any guy
who tries to talk to you, is gonna have to talk to me."
I glanced at my phone before putting it in my
pocket.
"Aw, so protective. Don't worry, I'm not worried
about a 'boyfriend' right now." I stretched my arms out and
hopped on his back.

I love piggyback rides from him.

"That's what they all say." he started walking around with me on his back.

"You don't think you'll get one?" I slightly smile. "A girlfriend I mean."

"Of course not." he propped me up on his back to keep me from slipping off. "What girl would wanna date a guy who looks like this?"

"Don't say that. Everyone will meet that special person SOMEDAY," I exaggerate.

"Sure, but maybe not me...Are you ready to get off? You're getting heavy."

"Oh yeah, sorry." I jumped down from his back, "You're just so tall and I needed a piggyback ride." I shrugged.

He laughed. "Maybe you're just so short."

"Haha," I said, getting irritated, "Seriously though...you never know who's out there that won't care about how you look; which honestly you look fine. I don't know if this is my place but I've been in this group for two years now and you've become like a big brother to me. All those times you comforted me in the funniest way when I was sad about my illness...but you need to have more confidence, Corey. That's why we're in this club, to help us cope with it and not let it affect our lives."

He looked down but I could tell he was thinking about what I said.

He looked back up at me. "Well, come on Bray, they're probably wondering where we are."

I sighed to myself and followed him out of the room.

43

Flashback Ends

Monday morning…

My alarm on my phone goes off and I wake up tapping the screen. It's 6:30 A.M. and it's time for me to get ready for school. School…I have mixed feelings about it. I love learning but man, I can't stand all the homework we are getting. I tiredly get out of bed and go inside the bathroom. After twenty minutes of being in there, I throw on a blue shirt with a flower in the middle, along with a blue, jean skirt, and a dark blue leather jacket. I put on some silver, flower earrings before applying mascara. I head to my mom's room so she can help me with my hair.

Her room is so big and comfortable. I used to want to sleep in here with her every night when we first moved here. She let me but eventually got tired of me and forced me to sleep in my own room. If my blood sugar goes low, I usually come to her room and end up falling back to sleep here anyway.

"Bailey not going to school today?" I ask.

"She's got a doctor's appointment…and they want to see her early for therapy today.

"Oh."

I really hope Bailey gets the chance to practice standing up and walking. She's in her wheelchair all day, every day.

But we are declaring Bailey's healing. She was born with cerebral palsy. Meaning she can't walk…not yet at least!

44

She finishes with my hair and I thank her. I go back into my room, grab my book bag and purse and head downstairs. I get my sisters' and my lunch out of the refrigerator and put it inside our book bags. I then make breakfast for my sisters and me and check my blood sugar. I give my insulin shot in my arm once I count the carbs to my food. As my mom comes down with Bailey, I bring her French Toast to her and we start eating. I put my shoes on when I'm done, and I grab my purse and head out the door. Then everyone else follows after getting everything they need.

"What was your blood sugar?" my mom asks.

"125...Oh, I gotta talk to you about something."

"What?"

"This boy I met at the party asked me out on a date."

"Okay...who is this boy?" she says, getting irritated. "You know you're too young to be going out on a date, Bray."

"I know, but he goes to my school and he's in the same grade as me," I say, getting worried. "I just wanna see how it goes...He seemed nice."

She rolls her eyes. "You can be friends and that's it."

"Mmmm...k," I say, irritated.

We arrive at the school twenty minutes later. I glance at the students getting dropped off and walking inside.

I get out of the car. "Bye you guys, bye Mom,"

"Byee," Bailey says.

"See you," Balice says.

45

"Alright see you," my mom says.

I walk into the school and go through security.

Today is the day that the Lord has made, I shall rejoice and be glad in it.

Heading up the stairs, I squeeze pass the big group of people standing at the top. I pull out my headphones from my jacket pocket and turn some music on.

"Hey Bray!" A group of people I know says.

"Heyy." I say, still able to hear them.

I get on the elevator to go to my first class. I get to use the elevator since I have a medical condition. Yippie. I walk down the long hall and go inside my classroom to see 3 people in there.

For once I'm early. I still have 30 minutes...Imma go down to the band room.

After getting off the elevator again, I arrive at the room. I tug on the door.

It's locked.

As I'm walking away, I hear the door open.

"Hey beautiful, trynna get it?"

Deep voice. Don't be nervous, Bray.

"Hey..." I turn around, "just wanted to check something on my violin...what are you doing?"

"Ms. Reds let me in here so I can straighten up the room before school starts. You're in orchestra?" Trey leans on the door.

"No. I bought a violin from the school 'cause I'm cool with the music teacher. It's technically her instrument because she bought it with her money but anyway, are you in the orchestra?"

"I was down here playing the piano a few days ago and Ms. Reds heard me and asked periodically if I could play with the orchestra," he says.

"You play the piano?"

"Yeah."

"That's cool...I've always wanted to play but can I help straighten up?"

"If you're sure," he says.

"I want to."

"Okay."

He holds the door open for me and I go inside. As we talk while cleaning, we get to know each other a little bit more. We laughed and got off track a few times, until the last 12 minutes were left.

He picks his book bag up off the floor. "How long have you played the violin?"

I stand in front of the piano. "3 years now."

"Is that all you play?"

"Yeah...I really wanna learn to play the guitar and piano though." I play lightly across the keys.

I look back up at Trey to see him walking towards me, not breaking eye contact. I can feel my heartbeat pick up speed as he stops in front of me.

He's so intimidating...but in a good way.

He sits his book bag down and steps even closer to me. He raises his hand.

Is he about to caress my cheek? I think to myself; but he presses on the keyboard and starts playing the keys.

"Here, press these three."

I grin while pressing them. "Oh really?"

"The guitar, flute, cello, drums, and harp…I can also play."

He presses on a few other keys and tells me to keep pressing mine.

"Must've had a lot of free time growing up."

"Parents wanted to keep me busy…I didn't mind though, I love music."

He plays more notes and finishes which makes me smile.

"Me too." I say quietly, "Loving the music part. Can you sing?" I turn to face him.

"What makes you think that?"

"Figured since you love music so much…and you kinda sound like you can, like, just the way your voice sounds. It seems like you can sing. If that makes any sense."

He laughs, "Yeah. I can."

"Let's hear it then."

"Naw, not today."

"Oh come on."

"One-day baby girl."

I take a deep breath.

"Fine." I whisper. "So…about the date. The thing is…my mom doesn't want me to date yet, but honestly, I think it's just because she doesn't know you."

He looks at me with a thinking expression.

"I wanna meet her," he says.

I look at him shocked. "What?"

"Yeah, I wanna meet her. Maybe she would change her mind if she met me."

"Today?"

He hunches his shoulders. "Yeah,"

"You sure?"

"Yes. I…I really wanna take you out and…I don't have any bad intentions with you or anything…but I'm just… starting to like you a lot."

I look at him.

Wow, not too many guys would admit that.

He looks into my eyes. "You know…if that's what you want."

I put my finger to my face and make a thinking expression.

"Hm? Is that what I want?"

He rolls his eyes. "Very funny,"

I laugh. "What's your lunch hour?"

"5th."

"Mine too."

"But I won't be there today 'cause I gotta make up for this test I missed." he says.

"Okay…well, class is about to start."

"Alright."

He takes my hand and we walk out of the room, going to
first hour.

At lunch…

"Hey nurse," I say, walking in as I sit on the nurse's bed.

"Hey Bray."

I take out my blood sugar pouch and check my sugar. I then go to the refrigerator and grab my insulin pin.

I grab a needle and go to the bathroom to take my shot. After I'm done, I come back in to find MJ checking her sugar too. Her hair is down in a kinky afro with her edges swooped. Her army fatigue pants match with her black shirt. The gold hoops she's wearing compliments the entire outfit.

"You look pretty, MJ."

She purses her lips. "Thanks, best friend, you do too, like always."

I thank her.

"...Bray, look...I got a new insulin pin."

"Is that Apidra?"

"Yeah, same as yours...my doctor wanted me to change pins just to see how everything goes," she takes her shot in her arm.

I nod and take a seat next to her.

"Wassup uglies."

I look to the door to see a long-time friend of mine, Chris. The only boy diabetic in the school.

"Shut up, peanut. Always calling somebody ugly." I smile as he playfully pushes me. "Why you coming down so late? Usually you're the first one."

"Sophomore assembly...mind yo business with yo nosy butt."

"Shut up, Chris. I can be nosy if I want to."

He looks at me and smiles.

"What was it, Bray?" Nurse Stone asks me.

"225 and I took 4 units."

She writes my recordings down in her book and looks at MJ, waiting for her to speak.

She puts her stuff away in her purse. "It was 408 and I took 9 units,"

"Ooo, that's high MJ," I say, concerned.

"Yeah ,I know, you know how my sugar is though. I went to the bathroom about 5 times…I knew I felt like punching somebody in class last period."

Chris and I say at the same time, "You always feel like that rather your sugar's high or normal, MJ."

"…true." MJ says.

I glance at her.

"Let me check for ketones real quick and I'll be right back."

We only have to check for ketones if our blood sugar is above 300. Checking for ketones means she has to pee in a cup, grab a ketone strip, place it inside the cup of pee, and wait a few seconds for the little square at the end of the strip to turn a color or stay light pink. There are different color stages if she has ketones. Light pink means zero ketones. Light purple is a little and dark purple is too much. Having ketones in our bloodstream is a huge no-no. It can just about cause us to go into a coma or kill us. What a life to live as a diabetic at just 14!

After a few seconds, she comes back and tells Nurse Stone that it was a small trace of ketones. She took her insulin already so it will bring it down. Nurse Stone nods and I say bye to Chris before MJ and I walk out and head to the lunchroom.

At Riverside High School after school.

Finally school is over.

I sigh and walk down the sidewalk with my friends.

"I swear if I get another homework assignment from Ms. Jones, I'm going to die, bro. Like for real, she is giving us too much work and it's hard as heck," says Alex.

"I mean she gave us two assignments in class and then gone come to our last hour to give more work. That's just petty cause like, she is the only teacher we got that's doing that. She is so irritating," MJ says.

"All I know is, I better get an A on this test Thursday, 'cause I've been doing everything she says," I say.

"What test?!" MJ yells out.

"Dang, you want the whole world to hear you?" I roll my eyes. "She said we're taking a test Thursday."

"Oh my gosh, we just started this topic though."

"I know, right? That's how teachers are these days."

"And that's exactly what I'm talking about," says Alex. "...I'll see y'all later."

"Byee."

I watch Alex's ponytail sway back and forth as she runs across the street getting into her boyfriend's car. Then suddenly, MJ's phone rings.

"Hello?" she answers her phone. "What do you mean you can't pick me up?! Okay so where's mom? Of course she is…You know what, whatever. Mom can come pick me up from Bray's house."

She hangs up and sighs in frustration.

"What happened?" I ask.

"Derion talking 'bout he can't pick me up from school 'cause he's getting out of work late and my mom is out with her drunk boyfriend, so she won't be able to get me until later."

She is so frustrated; you can see a vein popping out of her neck.

She looks at me with sincerity. "I'm sorry, but do you think your mom would mind?"

"No, of course not...let me call her right now."

I take out my phone and just as I was about to press my mom's name, I feel someone tap my right shoulder. I look but see no one. Then, I feel a tap on my left. I turn to look but see no one. Then again on my left and right. Getting slightly irritated, I spin around to the back to see Trey with a smile on his face.

"Hey, baby girl,"

"Hey, Trey," My annoyance is gone and is replaced with a wide smile.

Wait, dang Bray...don't smile so big. I clear my throat.

"MJ, this is Trey. Trey, this is my best friend MJ."

He shakes her hand. "Hey, nice to meet you."

"You too. So, you're Trey...you're cute." she smirks at me.

I look at her with wide eyes. "Really?" I whisper to her.

"Yeah." she whispers back. "His voice is...ooh girl!" she playfully slaps my shoulder.

I smile while shaking my head in amusement.

"Give me one moment, I have to call my mom," I tell him.

"Okay," he says.

I step over and tell my mom what happened with MJ.

"And Mom, there's someone who wants to meet you."

"Who?"

"The boy I was telling you about. His name is Trey."

I look over to see MJ and Trey talking.

She questions. "Why does he want to meet me?"

"To see if you'll let him take me out on a date."

"Well, that's a first…sure, bring him."

I grin. "Okay."

"Make your way towards me 'cause I'm here now."

"Alrighty."

I hang up and go back to my friends.

"She's here guys, let's go."

We walk to the car across the street to where my mom is parked. She gets out of the car and MJ gets in.

"Mom, this is Trey. Trey, this is my mom, Ms. Fletcher." I say.

Trey smiles. "Hi, it's nice to meet you, Ms. Fletcher," he holds his hand out.

She shakes his hand and says, "Hello, nice to meet you too."

"Well, I just wanted to say that your daughter has taken my attention and I would really like to take her out sometime, with your permission of course."

"Okay, and where to?" she asks.

I look at him.

"Movies, library, the park, ice cream shop, you know, like that."

She folds her arms. "What are your grades looking like?"

He smiles. "All As and I've gotten Bs a few times."

She sighs and looks at me. "Now usually I wouldn't let her go on dates...but it's fine with me if that's what she wants."

"Yes, it's what I want," I say, calmly.

"Okay then...and you said your name is...?"

"Trey."

"Alright, nice meeting you, Trey."

"Nice meeting you too Ms. Fletcher."

My mom goes back inside the car.

"That went well," he says.

"Yeah, better than I thought."

"So...you doing anything Friday night?"

I purse my lips. "Noppers, why?"

"Would you like to go on a date with me, Bray?"

I smile. "Yeah, that'll be great,"

He smiles at me. "Your mom is pretty."

I laugh and say, "Thank you, I'll let her know."

He scratches the back of his head. "Well, I'll see you tomorrow, and are we done using Snap Chat to text?" he chuckles a bit.

I laugh. "I'll text you my number later," I get into the car.

As I'm closing the door MJ stops me and yells out to Trey.

"Aye, Trey if you hurt Bray in any type of way...I'll be your Freddy Krueger." she smirks evilly.

"I believe you," he laughs. "But I won't." he looks at me.

55

I smile and close the door.

My mom pulls off. "He has some really pretty eyes,"

"I know, right?" I exaggerate.

"He's a handsome boy, Bray…and he had manners,"

"Yeah…and thanks, Mom."

"No problem."

"But really MJ? Freddy Krueger?" I laugh.

"Hecky yeah," she says. "I'll kick him where the sun doesn't shine," she whispers to me.

I shake my head.

"He said you're pretty, mom."

She smiles and turns on the radio.

MJ whispers in my ear. "Have you told him you're a diabetic yet?"

I shake my head.

"Why?"

"Because I don't wanna scare him off. Telling him hey, I'm a type 1 diabetic and I have to manage what I eat each day. I give myself shots every day, four times a day with two different pins and I prick my finger six times a day and give blood to this little device that calculates my blood sugar. I have mood swings depending on if my blood sugar is high or low. Also, diabetes is life-threatening if not taken care of properly, I can die at any time. So, if we're gonna be a 'thing' you have to kinda look out for me. But it's nice to meet you too." MJ giggles and I can't help but laugh with her.

She leans back in the seat. "We have one crazy yet interesting life,"

"Yeppers, we sure do."

I turn my head behind me to see the twins asleep. I laugh as I pull my phone out and take a picture of them.

Twenty minutes later, we finally arrived at my house.

Bailey pushes her wheelchair up the ramp and I unlock the door.

I take off my shoes. "Did you make any food today mom?"

She pops her gum. "Nope."

"That's not true…I smell chicken." I make my way to the kitchen.

She laughs and begins watching Bailey, carefully as she transfers herself out of her wheelchair and onto the couch.

"Wash yo hands before you touch anything." she says.

"Do you need any help?" MJ asks my mom.

"Aw no, thanks baby, but I'm fine. This one was supposed to help." she points to Balice.

"I can't. I had Bailey's book bag, plus my own and I had my violin." Balice says, getting frustrated. "Where's Bray, huh?"

I wash my hands and open the aluminum foil on the pot.

Ohhhh, it's pork chops…Pork chops and rice.

My mom comes in, starts fixing plates, and says, "That's all you think about is food."

"That's not true…I think about Jesus, ice cream, you, my sisters, and MJ too." I laugh. "Speaking of, where is MJ?"

"Bathroom."

"Oh."

"Tell Balice to come get her and Bailey food."

"Okay."

I walk into the living room to find Balice not there.

"Where's Bailce?"

Bailey takes her shoes off. "She went upstairs."

I walk over to the stairs and yell up to Balice that the food is ready.

"I forgot to ask you, how was therapy, Bailey?" I ask.

"It was okay."

Her long hair is in a messy ponytail. She tries reaching for the remote off the table. I notice and hand it to her.

"Did you walk or practice standing up?"

"Yeah, with a walker though." She changes the channel on the T.V.

"That's great!"

MJ comes down the hall from the bathroom, while Balice walks to the balcony of the hall, upstairs.

Balice looks down at me. "Tell mom I'll be down in a second."

"Okay, and she's making our plates now, MJ." I say.

She nods and we both walk into the kitchen.

MJ becomes cheerful. "Thank you so much Ms. Fletcher! This smells so good!"

"Aw thank you!"

MJ and I take out our meters from our purse and we check our blood sugar.

"I'm 205." I grab my insulin out of the refrigerator.

"I'm 336." MJ says. "Can't check for ketones because I just used the bathroom."

"Well, still make the correction with the food." my mom says.

"Okay."

MJ and I take our insulin shot in our arms and we walk into the living room to eat with Bailey. Balice walks in after and sits her plate on the small tray table. She has already changed out of her school uniform and has put her box braids into a bun.

"Can we please watch *How To Train Your Dragon?*" Balice asks.

"No, you always watch that." says Bailey.

In a playful sad voice she says, "But you guys haven't seen it in a long time."

"So what?"

"Baileeyyy…please." Balice says, getting irritated.

Bailey turns the channel to it. "Oh my gosh, Balice."

"Yay." Balice says.

MJ giggles. I grab the remote and press guide to see what else is on.

"Oh look, *High School Musical 2*." I say, looking at them.

"Let's watch it." Bailey says.

We all look at Balice.

"Oh, fine, turn it." she says.

I press the middle button and the movie is on the part when school just got out.

"What time is it, summertime…it's our vacation!" MJ jumps up and starts singing.

Bailey starts singing also "What time is it, summertime…that's right, say it loud."

Balice and I start singing too and soon enough we're dancing and yelling the words to the song. Eventually, Mom comes downstairs and joins us. We all shout the lyrics and laugh hard.

As the song goes off, we hear a knock on the door. My mom goes and opens it.

"I can hear y'all all the way outside." Brii says.

She rolls her eyes with a smile on her face.

We all try to catch our breath. "Hey Brii!" we all say, laughing.

"Where's Charlie?" mom asks.

"On the yard using the bathroom." she says.

She calls on Charlie to come inside the house. We all rub and play with him as he runs to us. We've had Charlie for a year now. He's a bichon frise and a shih tzu mixed. All white, curly fur.

Mom grimaces. "Get him off the couch, and y'all food is right there!"

We push him off and he wags his tail and runs around the room. Brii and Mom go into the kitchen. After twenty minutes, the twins and I finish eating and MJ and I go upstairs into my room to get started with homework.

MJ swings her book bag on the floor. "Girl, I don't feel like doing this right now."

I sit on my bed and take my notebook out. "Oh come on, it's not that bad."

"I'm just tired."

I giggle. "Well then you should've never been up so late."

"I wanna get out these clothes, do you mind if I borrow a shirt and stretch pants?" she asks.

"Naw, I don't mind."

She walks over to my dresser and takes off her shirt. Leaving her bra on. I glance at her and notice purple bruises on her lower back.

I hurry off the bed. "Oh my gosh, what happened, MJ?!"

She stops and looks at the dresser and mumbles something, but I couldn't quite catch what she said.

"Well?"

"Bray...don't worry about it...just some misunderstandings at home." She puts the shirt on quickly.

"No! That IS something to worry about. Someone's hurting you and I mean, hard too. It looks like someone hit you with a broom." I start to cry a bit. "Was it Derion?"

"No..." she says.

I look at her concerned. "Your...mom?"

She looks at me with tears in her eyes. I pull her into a comforting hug. She starts to cry and I touch her back lightly.

"But why?"

MJ pulls away from me. "She was mad that I went to the party...and after, she apologized like she's never done it before."

I look at her and sigh. "So this isn't the first time?" I feel my head boil with anger.

This is horrible! Maybe this is why MJ has been acting a little different...?

She rubs her face. "You know how we would get but whooping's when we was younger?"

I nod.

"This is her way of disciplining me when I talk back, or whatever. Sometimes she'll punch too…I try not to think about it too much."

I shake my head.

"When did THIS happen?"

She takes her glasses off. "Sunday night."

I sigh and put my hands on my hips. She puts her curly hair into a bun and sits on the bed.

"I guess this is what I get for sneaking out."

"Still don't make it right. My mom gets on me when I'm doing something wrong but she doesn't bruise me up…and with your condition, it's gonna take long for that to heal."

"I know. What time is it?" she asks.

I sigh and walk over to my nightstand.

I pick my phone up. "5:15." I grab the charger and hook it into my phone.

MJ looks up at the ceiling. "I know she doesn't mean to do it…she's got a lot going on right now and she doesn't need me disobeying her, and anyway this is only like the third time."

I sit on the bed and look at her. She looks up at me and I can tell from her eyes that she doesn't want to talk about it. I nod and she lays over and looks up at the ceiling again. I put my hands over my eyes and sigh.

"Bray don't worry…It's gonna be okay. Soon enough I'll be free from all of this."

I look down at her in confusion. "What do you mean?"

Just then, my mom walks into my room.

"Your mom is here, sweetie," she says.

MJ gets up and picks her bookbag up. I get up and put my things down. The three of us walk downstairs.

"Hey, MJ." Ms. Reeds says.

MJ says, "Hey Mom. Ms. Fletcher, thanks for letting me stay."

"You're welcome, sweetheart."

"Yeah, thanks again. I'll call you tomorrow, Bahati.

"Okay," my mom says.

I wave. "Bye MJ."

"See you Bray, and thanks."

I give her a sad smile and shut the door. I immediately hug my mom.

"What's wrong Bray?"

"Something's happening to MJ."

"What?"

I look up at my mom. "...She's getting beat at home."

"What? By who?"

"Her mom."

"Oh my God, Bray."

"Her mom's way of disciplining her...I just wish there was something we can do to help."

"I don't know, Bray. Come on, let's go to my room and pray for her."

"Okay." I say.

She hugs me while we walk upstairs to her room. We say our prayers and I go downstairs to make the twins and I lunch for school tomorrow. I headed upstairs to grab my phone and book bag and go back downstairs to watch T.V and do homework. I love watching T.V on this big, flat screen. After browsing through channels, I sigh when I find nothing on that I'd like to watch. I lay back on the couch and glance at my phone. I hesitantly Facetime Trey.

Don't be nervous. I sigh.

After a few rings, he answers.

I grin at him. "Heyy."

"Hey baby girl."

"What are you doing?" I ask.

"About to get started with homework. What about you?" he asks.

"Watching- uh, well, I can't find anything to watch."

"You alright? You seem kinda upset."

"I'm okay, just been thinking."

Thinking about MJ and her situation at home.

"Okay."

I change the subject. "Where are you planning on taking me?"

"Well that depends. What kind of stuff do you like to do?"

"Well, mostly everything you said is fine."

"Okay, tell me more about yourself." he says.

"Like what?"

"Anything."

"Okay. Well, I have three sisters and all of our name starts with a "B", even my mom's."

"Wow, what are they?" he asks.

"Brielle aka Brii, Bailey, Balice, and my mom's name is Bahati."

He smiles. "I bet your mom be calling y'all but mean the other...Bray-I mean, Brii, I mean, Bailey." He throws his head back in laughter and I laugh with him.

"All the time!" I say.

"What else?"

"I'm 14, my favorite color is blue. I want to be a dancer and actress when I grow up."

"Already knowing what you wanna do in life."

"I guess. Do you have any hobbies?"

"Yeah, actually I-"

As I position myself on the couch, I hear screaming and yelling come through Trey's phone.

"Is everything okay?" I ask.

"It's just my parents again...I'll have to talk to you tomorrow, sorry." he says, looking irritated.

"It's okay, I understand."

"It's not okay... Alright baby girl, see you tomorrow."

"Okay."

I press the hang up and go on Netflix to watch T.V for an hour. After, I head upstairs to Bailey and Balice's room to find them watching T.V. while playing with Charlie.

I jump on Balice's bed. "Hey y'all,"

She gives me a blank stare. "Don't do that." "What y'all watching?" I ask.

"*White Chicks.*" Bailey says.

I rub and pet Charlie as I glance up to see them both on their phone.

I roll my eyes. "Y'all always on ya phone. Y'all not even watching it."

Balice gives me the side eye. "It's on commercial,"

I pick up Charlie. "Y'all need to take y'all butts to sleep."

As I'm about to walk through the door Balice yells out, "What…? You had Charlie last night."

She scoffs and I walk out of the room. I take Charlie with me downstairs and give him a snack. Then I go to the kitchen, check my blood sugar, and I take my Lantus shot in my thigh. After that, I go upstairs to my room, carrying Charlie with me.

Mom shouts from her room, "BRAY."

"YES."

"DID YOU TAKE YOUR LANTUS?"

"YES…MY BLOOD SUGAR WAS 178."

"OKAY, JUST MAKING SURE. EAT SOMETHING ELSE, BRAY."

"I HAD A LITTLE CRUNCH, BUT GOODNIGHT." I place Charlie on my bed and get under my covers.

"GOOD NIGHT…TWINS, YALL BETTER BE ASLEEP OR ITS GONNA BE SOME TROUBLE. DON'T MAKE ME COME IN THERE."

I giggle as I hear them in the next room, scurrying to turn the T.V down and putting their phones on the charger.

"TOLD YALL," I say.

They both speak together. "SHUT UP."

I smile to myself as I drift off to sleep.
***

66

I feel a weird feeling course through my body -but mainly in my stomach- as I try to sleep. I toss and turn with that feeling growing more and more intense and I start to take deep breaths.

"My blood sugar…" the only thing I could think of. "But why would it be low?"

I glance over at my phone to check the time…it's 2:15 in the morning. I shoot up and find myself feeling dizzy. I quickly turn on my light next to my bed. Using alcohol to clean a finger, I prick it, and the meter carefully takes blood from my finger. After five seconds, it beeps a second time and reveals my sugar level to be 52. I thank God for waking me up as I reach out with my hand shaking tremendously, slowly grabbing my purse to get my ziplock bag of skittles and I get up, barely able to hold my balance and walk to my mom's room.

I shake her a little so she'll wake up.

"Mom…mom,"

"Hmm?"

"My blood sugar's 52."

"What?"

"It's 52."

She shoots up and asks me why and I tell her I didn't think it'd drop low because I ate candy before going to bed.

"But Bray, you know those things only have little carbs. You gotta at least make sure your sugar is in the 200s before going to sleep."

She's right. I should've eaten more candy but right now, I can't think clearly.

I shrug as I start eating 4 skittles. She watches me very carefully as I eat my candy. I slowly start to tip over.

"Bray are you okay?"

"Yeppers, just getting the symptoms…"

She looks at me with worry. "Wait 15 minutes and check it, Bray."

"Okay…can I stay in here?"

"Yeah."

I lie down. "If you go out…in the woods today…there's gonna be some frriiiieeess." I giggle, "hey, I never noticed the patterns on the ceiling." I raise my arm and trace the pattern with my finger. "Ha, weird…Noooo…I don't see another red skittle, mommy." She eyes me and I begin to fake a small cry. "The red skittle is my favorite…Haha I found one, WHOO!" my mom jumps from my outburst.

"Girl…eat your skittles."

After eating 11 more skittles, I get under the cover next to her and set a timer on her phone for 15 minutes as I wait for my blood sugar to rise up.

Chapter Four Friday

"With your right hand, you save me."
Psalm 138:7.

Friday morning…

The house is crazy this morning as we are trying to rush out. Once again, we are late. I look all around for my gold ring that my grandfather, Poppa, gave me. For some reason I can't find it! This is frustrating!

"CAN SOMEONE PLEASE FIND THE BRUSH."

"WE DON'T KNOW WHERE IT IS, BRII." Balice yells.

"YALL ARE SO IRRITATING." she yells.

I walk into the bathroom. "Whatever Brii."

Where is my ring?

I hear my mom say from her room, "Come on you guys, we're going to be late."

I walk into her room and say, "Mom, I can't find my ring," I sigh in frustration.

"That's on you Bray. You are always losing it."

I scan her room, finding the gold ring on the dresser.

I pick it up. "Ooh…found it."

Thank God.

She gives me an annoyed look.

"Thanks," I grin before walking out of her room.

"Finish getting ready and go downstairs, Bray!" she says.

"Okay…" I say, getting a little annoyed.

I go into my room and grab my things and head downstairs. I start to make my sister's and my breakfast and soon enough, Brii comes down with Bailey on her back. She sits her down on the chair and I give her her breakfast.

"Good luck with therapy today, Bailey," I say.

"You're not coming?" she asks.

I smile at her. "Noppers, I have a date tonight,"

"Really? Is it with that boy you were talking about in the car the other day?"

"Yeah, his name's Trey."

She smiles at me. "Ohh, I hope you have fun."

"I'm a little nervous."

"Don't be, Bray," Brii walks into the room. "Yeah, mom told me. I can't believe she's actually letting you go. If it was me, it would've been no from the start."

I shrug. "She did say no at first, but Trey wanted to meet her to change her mind."

Brii puts her shoes on. "He must really like yo ugly butt."

I roll my eyes and say, "I didn't even know you stayed over, Brii…you going with mom to therapy today?"

"Yeah…where Twin at?"

"Upstairs, I think." says Bailey.

"BALICE," says Brii.

"YEAH?"

"BRING DOWN MY CHARGER FOR ME."

"UH, FINE," she says.

70

Balice comes downstairs and hands Brii her charger.

I smile at Bailey and Balice. "Aw, y'all ACTUALLY look like twins today."

Both Bailey and Balice's hair are in a high bun with 1 braid hanging on each side and they both have a black uniform on with silver hoops. They look so cute.

Balice walks into the kitchen after saying, "Oh, shut up,"

I smile and put my shoes on. Mom comes downstairs and puts Bailey's shoes on.

"Bray, you still going on that date, right?" Mom asks.

"Yes." I say.

"So after school, I'm still going to pick you up and you'll still go to therapy with us, and then we'll come back here and get you ready."

"Oh, so I am going with y'all to therapy?"

She nods. I go into the kitchen and start eating my Nutella on toasted bread. I love Nutella on toasted bread.

"You checked your blood sugar, Bray?" mom asks.

"Yes...it's 225."

"Whyy?" she asks dramatically.

I shrug. "I don't know."

Waking up in the morning with a blood sugar level in the 200s isn't really good but I don't know why it's 225.

"Did you take insulin for that?"

"Yeah."

"Someone feed Charlie," Mom says.

Balice walks over to her book bag. "I already did."

"Alright guys, let's go."

71

We all put sweaters on and go outside.

"Come on, Charlie." says Balice.

We each get into the car and we say the Lord's Prayer. After 15 minutes we finally arrived at my school. I say goodbye to everyone and I go inside, heading to my first hour class. Once I'm in the classroom, I see Monia and Bekah.

"Hey Bray," they say together.

I go over and give them hugs. "Hey guys."

They hug me back and I sit down next to them.

"I haven't seen you guys at all this week! Where have y'all been?" I ask.

"Well, our moms wanted to take us to Kalahari before it starts getting cooler outside." says Bekah. "We've been there since Monday."

"That's cool." I pout. "I haven't been to Kalahari yet."

"Aw, maybe one day we can take you and MJ with us," Monia says.

"Yeah, that would be cool."

"How's everything with your club?" Bekah asks.

"It's okay, I guess. MJ and I have to come up with our colors."

"What about the diabetic color? It's blue, right?"

I take my folder out. "Yeah, I thought about that, but I don't know."

"Well, talk to MJ about it and see what she says," says Monia.

"Yeah."

Mr. Mathews says, "Okay everyone we're about to get started here...just let me pull up this computer."

"Hey Mr. Matthews, where you been at?" Lucas asks.

"Yeah, you missed the whole week." Monia says.

"Sorry, guys. My wife was in the hospital."

Concerned, Nya asks, "Aw, is she okay?"

"She'll be fine." he says.

"She'll be in my prayers." says Bekah.

We all nod.

"Thanks Bekah. My sons and I were really worried, but she's getting better."

"That's good." we all say.

I watch as Mr. Mathews breathes in deeply while closing his eyes.

I wonder if he's okay.

He's been my English teacher for the last 2 years.

"Okay, everyone I've got some good news. As you all know, my other job is reciting slam poetry. So I got us a field trip to go to my studio and meet a few other poets too. We'll be able to come up with one big poem, turn it into a song, and record it there."

Bekah squeals. "What? Oh my gosh, that is so cool!"

Redgy asks, "When is it?"

"October 25." Mr. Mathews states.

"We have to wait that long?" Jose says wearily.

I lower my eyes at him. "It's only in a few weeks."

"Yeah…too long." he says.

Mr. Mathews smiles. "My friend also suggested going to the candy shop down the street from the studio. They have some of the best."

"You always be talking about candy Mr. Mathews. Keep it up and you're gonna end up getting diabetes." Redgy says, brushing it off.

I shake my head and look down.

Flashback

Mr. Mathews raised his voice. "Alright, Alright, settle down class."

My 7th-grade class was loud.

I looked back at my work on the table.

Almost finished.

"I'm so ready for this class to be over." the boy said from across from me.

I looked up at the boy. He pushed his raven hair back while stretching out in his chair.

"Oooh can we get some of your candy Mr. Mathews?" I could hear a student ask from across the room even though the room was still noisy.

"Sure." Mr. Mathews said.

"You keep getting all this candy and you're gonna get diabetes. Did you hear me? You're gonna get DIABETES." the boy from across the room exaggerated.

My head turned to the person who had no idea what he was talking about. I continued to look at him as he said it once again.

He knows I'm a diabetic…why is he joking about that?

I turned my head away and looked down.

The boy in front of me yelled out. "HEY! YOU'RE OFFENDING SOMEONE OVER HERE! WHY DON'T YOU SHUT UP?!"

A few other people agreed and began to yell at him also. I looked at the boy in front of me.

He shyly smiles at me"Don't worry I got you."

and I thank him.

End of Flashback

I raise my head up and look at Redgy in disgust. Just about everyone in this class are the same people I went to middle school with.

"Don't say that, Redgy," Mr. Mathews says.

"That's not funny, Redgy," says Bekah.

"It's true," he says.

Irritated, I ask, "And how would you know?"

"Because that's how you get diabetes, from eating candy."

"It's not actually and unless you're a doctor or know somebody that has it, don't go around joking about something that's really serious and is life-threatening. Get your facts straight." I roll my eyes.

The whole class says. "Oooooooooooo."

"She told you." Maya says.

Redgy scoffs and shakes his head. I roll my eyes once again and look at Mr. Mathews, who's trying hard not to laugh. He looks at me and mouths, 'Are you okay?' and I nod while taking a deep breath.

Maybe that was too harsh. But he knows I'm diabetic...at least, it's been said when he was around.

There's a whole bunch of people who think the same as Redgy…if MJ was here, she probably would've slapped him.

"You mad or naw?" says Lucas.

Redgy scoffs. "Shut up."

"That's what you get, finally got yo butt told. Always talking mess."

"Okay guys, calm down."

"What were you 'bout to say?" Redgy stands up which makes Lucas stand up too.

"You heard me. You've been in the same class with Bray for the last 3 years. You know she's a diabetic you bu-"

Mr. Mathews yells. "Guys!"

Redgy starts getting close to Lucus's face and soon enough, they start cursing which led to them throwing hands. I watch as part of the class stand up from not wanting to be hit. Eventually, Mr. Mathews stops the fight and has other staff members send them to the principal's office.

"Now that that's over…here is an early permission slip to let your parents know about the trip," he says. He passes them out to Joshua first.

"This is a great opportunity for my poetry lovers…Bray, Bekah, Kayla, Thomas." he says, looking at us.

I give him a half-smile and say, "Yeah…I know I would enjoy this."

"Okay guys, take out paper and get started on the Do Now."

After class...

"Alright class, don't forget to get your permission slips signed and it's a five dollar fee." says Mr. Mathews.

When everyone clears the class, I go up to Mr. Mathews' desk.

"Hey, Mr. Mathews. I just wanted to make sure you're doing okay."

He types on his laptop. "Oh yeah, I'm great."

He glances up at me. I look into his green eyes and give him a blank stare. I watch as he runs his hands through his blondish, brown hair and he sighs.

"You know me too well, Bray."

"Well, you've been my English teacher since 7th grade, so...I can read ya like a map."

He laughs and says, "Yeah,"

I sit down. "So, what's going on?"

"Well, the reason why she's in the hospital is because...her mother passed and...my wife had a heart attack."

My eyes widened in shock. "Mr. Mathews, I'm so sorry."

He scratches his nose. "It's okay."

"But your wife is better?"

"Yes she is."

I give him a sad smile. "Well that's good. I'll keep her in my prayers."

"Thanks Bray."

"And if you need anything, just ask." I say, grabbing my bookbag. "I owe you anyway, from when you helped me through a hard time."

He nods then smiles.

"How has your diabetes been lately?"

"Up and down but I'm okay."

"Okay. See you Monday, Bray."

"You too."

I stand up while putting my book bag on before walking out to go to my next class.

At lunch…

I say to MJ. "They are always serving these nasty lunches."

"The salad is okay. Don't you have a lunch?"

"I always do but I wanted to try the salad."

I look to the side of me as Jason approaches. "Wassup MJ?"

Jason is another person who went to the same middle school as MJ and I. Are we fans of him? Not one bit.

MJ rolls her eyes. "Boy, get out of my face. You know I don't like yo irritating butt."

He puts his arm around her. "Come on girl, I don't be doing nothin'."

"This is exactly what I mean! Move!"

She pushes him off her.

He pouts. "You always mean to me."

MJ rolls her eyes. "Cause I don't like you."

I laugh and he looks at me.

"Wassup, Bray." he grabs my hand and smiles.

"Oh no. Move." I snatch my hand from him.

"Come on, my future wifey."

I give him a disgusted look.

"I thought I was your future 'wifey'," MJ says.

"Naw you're my future baby mama. Bray's the wifey though."

Oh my gosh, no he didn't.

Jason looks at MJ and back to me. "And for now, you know y'all my girlfriends."

"Bray already has a boyfriend." MJ says.

"Oh really? Who?" he scoffs. "I'll beat them up for taking what's mine."

"Them?" I ask, confused.

"Actually, she's not yours," a voice says behind Jason. I snap my head up and Jason turns around. The gorgeous Trey is standing behind him. He continues to look at Jason and then smiles.

"I'm Bray's boyfriend, but she doesn't 'belong' to anyone." Trey looks me up and down. He stands beside Jason, so they are now both facing each other. Jason looks between Trey and me.

He glares at Trey. "I think you have bad hearing. I just said they're BOTH MINE."

I know Jason is playing because he's had a crush on MJ and I since 6th grade but he's being way too serious now. What is wrong with him? Is he actually mad that I have a 'boyfriend' now?

Jason looks at me and back at Trey. I feel the tension rising as Jason balls his fist. Trey notices and smirks.

"Guess I hit a nerve."

Trey's face turns back serious as Jason tries to punch him but he dodges it. Trey balls his fist and I can see his muscles bulging. Trey takes a step forward as I step up and put my hand on his shoulder.

"Trey."

He relaxes and glances at me before glaring back at Jason.

"I suggest you get out of here." Trey growls.

Jason stares at me before walking off and saying, "This ain't over."

"I'm sorry. That was just petty," I apologize.

"He's weird like that," MJ says. "But dang, I would've loved to see a fight."

Trey and I both look at MJ.

"What?" she turns her direction to the front of the line.

Trey smiles at me and I finally have the chance to actually look at him. His green shirt is literally the same color as his eyes. He's wearing loose, black jeans and has a cross chain around his neck. He looks handsome.

"I'm sorry I said I was your boyfriend I- I just wanted to prove a point. Not saying that I don't, want to be your boyfriend. I do- I…" he stutters.

"You're fine Trey." I smile and he blushes.

Why is he blushing?

"But…Hey." he chuckles, giving me a hug.

I laugh. "Heyy." I hug him back. I can see the girls in line staring at Trey.

"Hey MJ."

She laughs. "Hey Trey."

I smile at him. "I'm so excited for tonight."

We interlace hands and he says, "I'm glad you're excited…I'm happy too."

80

We look into each other's eyes for what seemed like forever before I turn my head in a direction where a group of girls are glaring at me not too far from the lunch line. Trey looks too and back at me.

"Don't worry about them. They just have a little crush on me."

"You've met them?" I ask.

"Only two of 'em…but the rest of 'em came up to me and started flirting with me the first week of school. I turned them all down."

I look up at him and then at the girls.

"Yeah 'cause if they keep staring, Imma say something to them." MJ says getting annoyed. "Is that Tyler?"

I look over to see Tyler whispering something to one of the girl's ears and then laugh. I roll my eyes at her and say, "Probably jealous again."

"You know Tyler?" Trey asks.

"Yeah, you?"

"Yeah, I got a class with her…I'm guessing you guys aren't friends?"

I let go of his hands. "No, not anymore."

He looks at me concerned. "What's wrong?"

"Nothing."

I try to hide the fact that I'm mad.

I'm mad at the fact that she met him in the first place.

"She did something to you?"

"…I'll tell you one day."

"Okay." he puts his arm around my neck. "You good?"

81

"Yeah. I'm not about to let that ruin my day."

"Okay," he smiles.

I can't stay mad with that perfect smile of his.

I look over at Tyler to see her arms crossed and eyes narrowed. Trey looks at her and I giggle as he whispers something in my ear.

MJ smiles. "You guys are too cute."

After school in Ms. Burch classroom...

"See you Monday, Bray," Bekah says.

"Okay, bye." I wave before putting my notebook in my bookbag.

As I put the rest of my things in my bookbag, I realize that someone else is still in Ms. Burch's classroom. I look up to see Tyler staring at me with her arms folded. She's wearing another Dior shirt.

Tyler walks towards me. "So I see you're with Trey now."

"That's none of your business." I get up, heading towards the door.

"I saw how you guys were all over each other. I mean you two were practically ready to risk it all at lunch today."

No we weren't...

I roll my eyes and say, "Why? Because he had his arm around me? At least I don't throw myself at a guy who doesn't want me."

Tyler shrugs. "I'm just surprised. Considering the fact that you're ugly, barely have hair-"

I turn around to see her caress her long brownish, blonde hair. "-And you look like someone's Aunt.

Do I really? Is looking like Auntie a bad thing? Dang, I guess it is.

She continues, "Can't believe you're the girl he kept gushing about. You're not that pretty." She walks closer towards me.

I glare at her. "You know what, Tyler? I could care less about what you're surprised at. From the fact that this has happened before...-YOU being jealous of ME- you should try to change your ways and do better for yourself. But, I guess you haven't changed."

"Oh? That's not what people are telling me." she says.

"Of course. 'Cause they don't know the real you. But I do. Now, if you'll excuse me, I have a date to get ready for."

I give her a fake smile and walk out the door. I can hear her sigh in frustration.

Can't believe I was best friends with her.

I take the elevator down to the first floor and walk out the door to find MJ waiting for me.

She hugs me. "Hope you have fun with your date tonight."

I hugged her back. "Thanks, MJ."

Just thinking about the date is making me nervous.

"Tomorrow at the hospital, you gotta tell me everything, okay?"

"You already know I will."

"Hey Bray, hey MJ." I look at Kyle as he walks past.

I wave. "Hey."

"Wassup, Kyle," MJ says.

Suddenly, my phone starts to ring. I look at my phone and answer it. "Hey Mom, I'm almost to you." I hang up the phone and pick my pace up.

MJ smiles. "Alright, it looks like my brother's here. I'll see you tomorrow, Bray."

"Alright bye."

We do our handshake before she runs across the street and I go to my mom's car and get in. We head downtown to take Bailey to physical therapy. After therapy is over, we go back to our house to get me ready.

"You nervous?" Mom asks me.

"Yeah, I am...Should I be?"

"Well, I guess. But don't be, Bray."

"When was your first date?" I ask her.

Mom smiles, putting eyeshadow on me. "I was 15. I went to this place called 'The Butterfly' and I had a great time. It was a place where it was pool, go karts, video games and stuff like that."

"That's so cool mom."

"Did he tell you where you were going?" she asks.

"No, actually. He said it's a surprise." I say.

She grabs the mascara. "Oh really?"

"Yeppers," I say.

"Well, call me and let me know where you'll be."

"Okay. What time is it?"

Mom looks at her phone. "6:53. What time will he be here?"

"7:00," I say.

"You still haven't told him you're a diabetic yet, have you?"

"I will tonight."

"Usually, you would have said something by now. Why haven't you?"

"I don't know…" I say honestly.

Now that I think about it, I could have told him but I just haven't.

"Okay Bray…well, you're done now. You look very beautiful."

I smile at her.

"Thank you so much, Mom, for letting me go."

"You're welcome, Bray. I trust you, so it's okay."

I smile at Mom and give her a hug. I go into the twin's room and we give each other hugs as they tell me they hope I have a good time. I then go into Brii's room.

"Well it's almost time, Brii…Ooh I'm so nervous! I hope I have fun!"

"You will, Bray. Don't worry about it. Come here, give me a hug.

I walk towards her and hug her.

"How do I look?"

"You look cute."

I thank her.

"No kissing on the first date Bray," she playfully pushes me over. "I will murder you."

"Of course, Brii." I say, shocked.

She side eyes me. "Mhmm."

I scrunch my eyes at her as she focused her attention back to her phone.

Mom calls from downstairs. "BRAY, TREY'S HERE."

"COMING. Alright, see you later Brii."

"Alright, Bray. Have fun."

"Okay."

Before walking out of the room, I look at myself one last time before walking downstairs.

I straighten my light pink, floral dress and I tug at the hem of my light pink leggings, pulling them down a bit. I twirl and watch as my dress flares out.

I love this dress.

I walk out of my bedroom before turning the lights off. I go downstairs to find Trey and my mom at the door.

Trey looks me up and down. "You look really pretty."

"Thank you. You look really nice too."

"I, uh, brought you some flowers. I know how much you love them since you're always wearing floral patterns." He hands them to me.

"Wow, thank you, and you're right. I do."

I smile as I sniff the flowers.

"Thank you." I say again, looking into his eyes.

My mom says, "I'll put them in water for you, Bray," I hand them to her. "Alrighty…have her back by 9:00, sir."

"Yes mam." he says.

To me, she asks, "You got all you need?"

I grab my purse from the table. "Yes, it's all in my purse."

The three of us walk out to the car and my mom and Trey's mom talk. After they finish, Mrs. Williams goes back inside the car.

My mom hugs me. "Okay, have fun."

I give her a kiss on her cheek. "Alright, love you mom."

"Love you too, Bray."

Trey smiles. "Bye, Ms. Fletcher."

"Bye, Trey."

Trey holds the door open for me as I get inside the back seat of his car. He gets in, sitting beside me and his mom pulls off.

Chapter Five The Date

"Every good and perfect gift is from above, coming
down from the Father of the heavenly lights, who does not
change like shifting shadows."
James 1:17.

After being in the car, we drive twenty minutes
away from my house to my favorite restaurant JayR's.
JayR's is a popular restaurant in Mexican town. My family
and I would just about eat there every week. We slowly
pull up and I look out the window to see people dancing to
the music playing. I smile widely at the sight of it.

Trey opens the door for me. "I thought this would
be fun to go to since this is how we met,"

I smile at him and say, "This is one of my favorite
restaurants."

"Well, you did tell me you used to live in Mexican
town."

"How'd you even know this was going on?" I ask.

"I got a flyer a few days ago when my mom and I
were driving around. It was packed, too. Luckily, the
cashier told us about the dance parties at night here."

I smile to myself.

"This is really cool, Trey."

He looks at me and smiles.

"Okay guys, I'll be inside ordering my food," says
Mrs. Williams.

"Okay…it looks like they have some food out here too, mom," Trey says.

"Well, just come in when you guys get hungry," she says, grabbing her purse. "Here's some money if you guys want face painting."

"It's okay, I have some," he says.

She gestures to the money. "You sure?"

"Yeah, thanks though."

"Okay. See you guys in a bit…and Bray? Watch him, okay?" She laughs as she walks away.

I laugh while Trey takes my hand and leads me where everyone is dancing. We start to dance together and soon enough, the 'Countdown Hustle' comes on.

Trey bites his lip. "Uh, you gotta know this dance!"

I raise my eyebrow. "Of course I do!"

I look around to see everyone in formation to start the dance. We all started dancing and I was actually shocked to see Trey doing it. As I'm dancing, I see Trey smiling widely at me and I can hear people yelling and screaming. Soon enough, the music goes off and I start laughing while catching my breath. People then crowded towards the middle, squishing Trey and I. Everyone starts jumping up and down, the two of us. We try to squeeze through people to leave the crowded section. Trey takes my hand and we finally manage to get out of the crowd.

I giggle. "You really can dance,"

He laughs. "Told you, baby girl."

I put my arms around his neck. "I can say, though, you were a little off on your turns."

He looks at me like I've grown two heads. "Uhh who told you that?" he raises his eyebrows.

89

I smile. "I told myself."

He puts his arms around my waist. "Now you know that I killed those moves."

"Mhm okay…you were great."

"You were too," he says.

He continues to hold on to me and pulls me toward him. I giggle and look him in his eyes as butterflies fill my stomach. I turn my head away from him, with a grin on my face. I try to playfully pull away from him.

He laughs. "You tryna get away from me?"

I put my hands on his chest. "Yes 'cause I want to get my face painted."

"Alright."

He lets go of me and we head to the face painting section. As we wait in line, we take our phones out and get on Snapchat. We post pictures of both of us and take videos of each other. After 5 minutes, it's finally Trey's and my turn.

I ask him. "What should we get?"

He thinks and whispers in the artist's ear. After two minutes, she finishes, and Trey reveals my name on his cheek.

Cheesy…just cheesy.

I tell the artist to paint *Trey* and she finishes in the same amount of time.

"You ready to eat?" he asks.

I stand. "Yes, please."

We both go inside the restaurant to find Trey's mom eating and texting on her phone. She points at our table which is 2 tables away from hers. He pulls the chair out for me and I take a seat. I thank him and he sits across from me. We pick up the menus and start looking at them

"What do you think so far? It's, okay?"

I smile. "Yeah, this is great."

These are the kinds of parties I love. A place where I can be myself without judgment. I can dance incredibly or terribly and I would still have a great time.

He smiles.

I squeal. "I feel like I'm in a movie."

He turns his head sideways, with a soft smile on his face.

"The whole dance party outside reminds me of the first movie of *Step Up*. The party dance scene."

He nods. "You said you like acting, so…big movie fan, aren't you?"

"Yeah, I love them."

Then, the waiter comes and greets us.

"What type of drinks will you be ordering this evening?"

"Mountain Dew."

"Diet Coke please." I say.

Diet pop has no carbs or sugar. I mostly drink it when I go to restaurants. I haven't had regular pop in so long that I don't think I could tell the difference.

"Okay, I'll give you guys a few minutes to look over the menu."

"Thanks." I say.

"Thank you." Trey says.

He leaves and comes back with our drinks.

He smiles. "All genres…of movies?"

"Yeah, but only certain scary movies. I love psychological horrors. I can't do some paranormals…and some slashers are fine, but ain't no way I'm watching it alone. I get over-dramatically scared."

He laughs.

"Like yelling at the T.V scared and jumping and laughing afterwards.

"I'm a huge fan of scary movies. We're gonna have to see one soon so I can laugh at you."

I scoff, "How dare you?"

He chuckles. "Don't worry, you can cuddle up with me if you get scared."

I raise my eyebrows. "Whatever, Trey." I shake my head.

"Come here."

We both lean across the table.

"You're gonna have to help me with the food 'cause I have no idea what to get."

I can't help but laugh hard at what he says.

"Don't laugh. I've never had Mexican food before from a restaurant."

I finally stop laughing.

I say, "I love the flaky tacos and rice, but the chicken and steak quesadillas are good. The enchiladas, and the taco salad ia slap."

He blinks. "Alright baby girl, we'll get it all."

"Really?" I ask.

"Yeah, my mom doesn't really know what to get either. She chose anything. She texted me when we were getting our face done, like, '*I don't know what to get from here*'."

I giggle.

"Plus, I wanna try it all."

"If you say so, but you won't be disappointed."

He mocks me. "If you say so."

I shake my head as he licks his lips while looking at me. Then, the waiter comes and takes our order.

"So, what's that thing you have to do on Saturdays?"

I take a sip of my coke before speaking.

Okay...the conversation I wanted to have.

"I'm in this group called the National Illness Club."

"What's that?" he asks.

"It's a club at the hospital for people with different illnesses." I say.

"What illness do you have?"

"I'm a type 1 diabetic."

"Really? Wow. I'm so sorry."

"Not your fault, but on Saturdays from 12 to 2, that's where I be."

"I feel like hugging you right now."

I grin at him. "Cheesy."

"I know."

I smile and take a sip again.

"My grandfather has diabetes too...he just be eating anything." he shakes his head.

"Aw, I'm sorry to hear that, Trey."

"It's okay. He knows how to take care of himself."

"That's good then. He technically can eat anything he wants, just smaller portions depending on the carbs." I smile at him.

Trey opens his straw. "So tell me more about the National Illness Club."

"Well, MJ was the one that told me about it and I joined 3 years ago-

"Wait, MJ's in it?"

I nod.

"For...? If it's okay that I'm asking."

"No it's fine. She's a diabetic.

"MJ's a diabetic too?"

"Yeah, we met at diabetic camp."

"Where's the diabetic camp?"

"In Fenton, Michigan."

"Oh."

"She was in the group already and she helped me a lot with coping with it and told me about the club on Saturdays...that it would help me even more. So when I started going, we became best friends, and the people there were really nice and I fell in love with it. So MJ and I got the idea of starting our own club, which will be soon."

"Wow...that's really awesome. So, if you don't mind me asking, what's it like being a diabetic? I know it must be hard."

I pause for a second. I haven't been asked this question in a long time.

"Well, to be honest, it's still kind of hard for me to believe I am one sometimes. I didn't even know what it was, and to find out that I got it out of nowhere...it was hard."

He nods his head in understandment.

"But I have to check my blood sugar six times a day. Meaning I have to prick my finger and give blood to a device that calculates my blood sugar. It can sometimes be more than six times. I have to take insulin shots four times. One each for breakfast, lunch, dinner, and one at night while I'm sleeping. Then I also have to take a shot depending on my blood sugar after I eat or if it's just high, all while going through these crazy symptoms from it being high or low" I say, shaking my head. "Also, I take longer to heal if I get cut or bruised and…complications with my skin, my hair," I sigh, trailing off.

He looks down for a second. "You're type 1?"

"Yeah,"

"So what's the difference from type 2?"

"Type 2 is usually found in adults, but it occurs if you're overweight and it's when the pancreas doesn't make enough insulin. Whereas type 1 is when the pancreas makes no insulin and is found in children. I got it when I was 11."

"So is there a difference between it being high or low?"

"I think having your sugar low is worse than it being high. When it's high, you may have an increased thirst for something to drink, and use the bathroom every five seconds, and get a nerve-wrecking headache and have a lot or no appetite at all when it's high, and yes, it's life threatening because sometimes I can't breathe. But I'd rather get that than this unexplainable feeling I get when there's hardly no sugar in me. My hands start shaking, I become sweaty, and dizzy and confused. I sort of act a bit weird, I guess. I be so close to passing out, I think I might one day…and it's also life threatening…I could have a seizure and go into a coma. So I would rather it be normal." I laugh.

He gives me a sad smile.

"Ya know, that's a lot, going through all of that. You're really brave, Bray."

I smile at him. "No one's ever told me that before…"

"They will."

As we sit talking, I tell him about everyone in the group. How we're all close friends, how MJ likes Ty, and how close Kevin and I are.

I take a sip of my pop. "Now it's your turn to tell me more about yourself."

"Well, I play basketball…like ever since I could walk." I smile as he continues, "I love to dance and um…I like reading books."

I smile. "You do?"

"Yeah…and I'm kind of a nerd, I'm really dedicated to school."

I giggle a little and say, "Just because you're focused on school doesn't make you a nerd."

"I guess you're right…"

"I'm always right."

He raises his eyebrow. "Cocky?"

"Yup."

He laughs, showing his perfect white teeth. I smile as he locks eyes with me.

"I'm 15, as you already know. I have a younger sister…she's 8 going 18. I love any type of music and when I grow up, I wanna be a singer and a poet. And no matter what anyone says,"

He leans in and I do too.

"...'Napoleon Dynamite' will always be my favorite movie."

I laugh.

"Oh my gosh! I love 'Napoleon Dynamite.'"

"Right? That movie is hilarious."

"What about 'White Chicks' or 'Fist Fight'?"

"Aw don't even get me started on those two." he says, laughing.

After about 15 minutes of talking and laughing, the waiter comes back with our food. I tell Trey that I have to go take my medicine and he nods as I walk to the bathroom.

This date is literally going perfect, almost too good to be true…133…that's good.

I calculate how many carbs I'm eating and look at my card to see how many units it will be. I take 5 units in my arm. I call my mom and let her know where I am and what my blood sugar is. After hanging up, I look at myself in the mirror to make sure nothing's on my face.

Lord please let this be a good date…I think I really like this boy.

I smile to myself and head out the door. As I make my way back to the table, I notice Trey's mom not sitting at her table.

"Where's your mom?"

"She went to the car."

"Oh." I say.

"Everything okay with your sugar?"

"Yeah, everything's good."

I sit down and we start to eat.

"What do you think?" I ask him.

He chews and makes a face like he's thinking real hard.

So silly.

"It's good." he finally says.

He takes another bite of the taco and I take a bite of mine. I have a great time talking with Trey as we talk about the most random things.

Our favorite cars.

"Mine's a Bentley and Mustangs." he says.

"Well, mine's a Camaro and an Escalade." I say.

Pet peeves.

"I honestly can't stand when my food touches, like I can't STAND it. And I'd eat anything, says my mom but my food cannot touch." I shiver.

He smirks for a few seconds before his facial expression changes in an instant.

"I can't stand bugs."

"Oh my gosh, finally someone understands! I jump from ants, okay?" I say, dramatically.

"Especially when there's just too many of them in one space." He makes a disgusted look and I laugh.

He runs his fingers through his curly hair. "Don't ever take me camping."

Our favorite shows.

"Mines 'Wild n' Out'." he says.

"My favorite show is 'The Flash'."

"Oh yeah, I've heard of that. Never watched it though."

I purse my lips. "It's good. Every genre in one."

"We'll have to watch it then." he purses his lips.

98

"Yeah and many episodes of 'Wild n' Out…maybe someday in the future, we could watch it with my family."

"Maybe." he smirks.

And our fears.

"I'm actually claustrophobic." he says. "Been trying to overcome it, it's just hard.

"I understand. I kind of have trypophobia. It's more of a disgust when looking at small holes or clusters of it together. Like what you said about the ants being in one place together, to me it would be so disgusting to look at…but I'd be afraid if I stopped loving God. I mean because of Him I've gotten through so much and I just hope that I would always keep believing in Him even when things are at the worst it's ever been." I stare at my plate.

"Even if you did, He'll show you how to love him again." he smiles lightly.

I smile softly, believing him. "I'm guessing you're a religious person." I set my head on my hands.

"Yes and I'm not afraid to admit it. I believe that God placed us on this earth for a reason and I think in order to survive we have to follow His Ten Commandments to help us be with Him in the end."

Perfect, he's perfect.

"…I can't agree more." I smile at him. "I'm very religious myself."

He nods. "That's good." he licks his lips..

I smile as we start to eat again.

After about 40 minutes, Trey's mom comes back inside and by that time we're finished eating, so we decide to go back outside. It's dark now but the lights hanging around make it bright and pretty outside. I gasp as one of my favorite songs comes on.

Trey looks at me with amusement. "You like this song?"

"One of my favorites!"

"What are we waiting for then?"

We interlace hands and head towards the group of people slow dancing. He spins me around and pulls me close as and we dance under the pretty, decorated lights hanging above us. I smile at the sight of it. I bring my eyes back down to him. As I look up at him, everything around us disappears and it's as if we're the only people in the world. He looks down at me. What movie am I in right now? This can't be real.

What is this feeling I'm getting?

"You're so short, Bray." he laughs.

I pull away from him, about to walk away. He grabs my hands, bringing me back towards him chuckling.

He says with a smile still on his face, "Don't walk away."

I smirk, shaking my head. "You ruined the moment."

"You're different than most girls, baby girl."

And he made it perfect again.

"Well you know what they say. Diabetics are naturally sweet." I put on a fake smile.

He throws his head back in laughter and I laugh with him.

"That was cute."

I blush and look down.

"You're cute when you blush." His laugh fades a little. "And have I told you how much I love your short hair?"

I look back up at him.

"It's different." he caresses it. "And I like it."

I smile at him. "Thank you."

"You're welcome."

I rest my head on his chest as I put my other arm around his neck, and he puts his around my waist. I sniff his scent.

He smells so good.

"So…" he says after a few minutes.

I raise my head up to look at him.

"How was our first date? I did okay?" he asks.

"Well, let's see…you brought me to one of my favorite restaurants, there's like a whole block party right here, by the way-one of the best parties I've been to in a while-".

He smiles as I continue.

"I got a taco today. I got my face painted and you brought me flowers." I smile with adoration. "But most importantly, I got to know you more. So I'd say…it was 'okay'."

He raises his eyebrow and shakes his head while smiling.

"I'm joking…it was perfect."

He looks at me with devotion.

"Good, 'cause I've been meaning to ask you," he says.

"What?"

"To make this official…will you be my girlfriend?"

I look down.

"Sure that's what you want?" I look back up at him.

"Heck yeah, that's what I want."

I smile and nod slowly.

"Then, of course I'll be your girlfriend."

He smiles widely as he spins me around and we dance 'till the song ends.

Chapter Six Diabetes
09/23

"So do not fear for I am with you; do not be dismayed for I am your God. I will strengthen you and help you.I will uphold you with my righteous hand."

Isaiah 41:10.

At Lakeside Hospital...

"He asked you to be his girlfriend?"

I run my fingers through my hair. "Yeah."

MJ's voice comes from inside the stall. "Did you say yes?"

"Yeah...I was a little hesitant though...I'm actually thinking of breaking it off."

She flushes the toilet. "Why?"

"I stayed up last night thinking about it."

"Did something happen on the date?" MJ opens the door and begins washing her hands.

"No, the date was perfect. He was perfect...It's just, this is my first boyfriend, and I don't know if he'd be able to..."

"To what?" MJ asks.

"To- to actually be..."

"With you?" she looks at me concerned.

"With everything that's going on with me…I always thought no one would ever want to date someone with-

She walks closer to me. "Bray. You can't think like that."

"But it's true. He'd have to be on the lookout every single second just to make sure nothing happens to me from my blood sugar. I'd be a burden to him because with certain situations, I can't do everything. I'd be better off being with someone that's also fighting an invisible issue." I feel myself get teary eyed and I face myself back towards the mirror, with my head down.

"Bray. Listen to me. I know exactly how you feel. But the only reason you're saying that is because of that butthole back in the summer. He said that he wouldn't want to date a girl with diabetes, while he was at a diabetic support group. I can't stand ignorant people…you can't let that get to you…and Trey doesn't even seem like that type of person. You like him, don't you?"

I look back at her and nod.

"And I can tell from the way he looks at you that he really likes you too. So, give him a chance and see how it goes and if he gives out and says that he doesn't want to be with you anymore 'cause he can't handle it, then that's on him and he wasn't worth it."

I wipe my tears and nod.

"Come here." she pulls me into a hug.

"Thanks, sis." I say.

"You're welcome, boo." We pull away. "Now get your emotional butt to the room." she curses, and I laugh. "Getting tears on my back and stuff."

A few minutes later…

"Wait…you went on your first date and didn't tell me?!"

"Well I wasn't even sure I was gonna be able to go because of my mom saying no."

Rachelle asked, "Wait, your mom said no?"

"Yes…but then Trey asked to meet her and that changed her mind."

Rachelle smiles all hopelessly. "Awww, that is so cute."

"So tell us exactly what happened." says MJ.

"Well, he took me to my favorite restaurant, JayR's and they were having some type of outside party. So we danced, we ate, got our face painted and talked about random things." I begin to daydream.

"Is he cute?" Rachelle asks.

"Way better than cute!" I say, getting hyper.

"Yeah if you saw him, you'll say the same." says MJ.

Rachelle laughs as I start to blush.

"I can't help to overhear," Chanel says, "But who are you guys talking about being cute?" She's walking over to us, flipping her straight hair. Her eyebrows are arched and filled in. Her eyelashes are enhanced and the dark nude on her lip compliments her outfit. She and I are kind of matching with our sweater shirts and jeans.

Chanel gives me a hug and I hug her back. I pull away and she sits on my lap.

"You look cute today," she states.

"You do too." I tell her.

"But who's cute?"

"Bray's new boyfriend," Rachelle says.

"You got a boyfriend now?" she asks.

"Yeah...I do."

Woah, I have a boyfriend.

"Got a picture of him?"

"Yeah."

I take my phone out and go on Snapchat to a picture of us and I show Chanel and Rachelle.

I really should change my case. I've had this light blue case for the longest.

"He's handsome." Chanel says.

"Oooh girl, he is." Rachelle says. "You're so lucky."

I half smile as I press my power button.

Chanel looks down at me. "I hope he ain't playing with you."

I look up at her as she continues.

"Just know you can't trust these boys because he still is...a boy. And with your condition, he'll never truly understand what you go through...and he'll take it for granted."

I lower my eyes and look down as I think about a time where Nurse Belsh held a lock in for the club.

Flashback

At Lakeside Hospital 12:43 a.m

I woke up to the sound of yelling and screaming. I shuffled around in my sleeping bag trying to go back to sleep. Hearing glass break, I snapped my head up to see Chanel being held by two nurses. I looked around to see a few members from the club, slowly waking up, and the rest were watching from a corner.

"Chanel! Chanel! Cha-

Chanel continued to scream out and struggled to get out of the nurse's grip. I watched in horror as Chanel was injected with something and carried out of the room. When I looked around, I saw Kayla at the far back of the room and at first, I was confused as to why I saw Kayla and not Ty. Then, I remembered that the guy's are all sleeping in the other room. I walked to her as she wiped tears from her eyes.

I wiped my tired eyes. "Kayla, what happened?"

"I can't tell you."

Her curly hair was in a puff ball before she quickly took her hair out and massaged her scalp.

I looked at her confused and slightly annoyed. "You can't tell me?"

She glared at me. "That's what I just said."

"Oh my gosh, can you stop being the mean girl for a second and talk to me?! I literally just watched someone I care about being carried out of this room."

She looked at me, rolled her eyes and folded her arms.

This girl...

After about 30 seconds, she sighed and unfolded her arms.

"This guy she was dating- well, kind of dating...or so she thought...he um...he leaked a picture because he thought she was so called 'cheating' on him."

"Oh, no..."

"And her dad, he...basically wants nothing to do with her, and she loves him so much."

I was on the verge of tears.

"I wish I could go punch that jerk." she sniffed and balled her fists. "He needs a good beating on that as-"

Rachelle appeared. "Guys, Nurse Belsh said she wants to talk to us."

"Okay." I said and looked back at Kayla.

"Come on," she said and I put my arm around her and she did the same while we walked back to everyone else.

Flashback Ends

"Just letting you know from experience." Chanel gets off my lap. "I just don't want to see you get hurt."

I look back up at her as she leaves and goes over to Mary-Kate. I look over at MJ and she whispers, "Remember what I said." I nod.

Ty and Kayla walk in as Nurse Belsh says, "Okay everyone, gather around, I've got some good news." I go over and take a seat next to Corey as Kevin sits on the other side of me. We all say hey to each other as everyone else grabs a chair and sits down.

"So as most of you know, it's time for the hospital's annual carnival fundraiser and I just want to make sure everyone will be able to come."

"Wait…what carnival?" Mary-Kate asks.

I tell her, "The hospital hosts a carnival every year to raise awareness and also hosts fundraisers for more medicine, different equipment for special needs, and for this group."

"Oh wow, that's cool. When is it?" Mary-Kate asks.

"Next Saturday," Nurse Belsh tells her, "We're trying to get a field trip to go to Children's hospital to have a little fun day with the kids there."

"When will that be?" Kayla asks.

"In December." Nurse Belsh says.

Kayla says, "Those carnivals be the funnest event ever…and at night, they play a movie screening for everyone. So you can sit on the grass and watch it."

Nurse Belsh begins passing out flyers. "So just make sure to let your families and friends know. Everyone is welcome to come, and there's no charge to enter but only for the food and games."

I smile as I look at the flyer. "You guys change it up every year."

She smiles at me and hands one out to the last person.

"Thinking about coming this time, Corey?" I ask.

"I don't know. You know I don't do so well around people."

"I think you should come. Don't think about what other people will say."

He gives me a little smile. "We'll see."

Kevin leans toward me. "Got anyone you're gonna be bringing with you this year, Bray?"

His blue shirt is complimenting his blue eyes.

"Yeah I do, and you know, of course, my family."

"Yeah."

"Okay guys, for today, we will be discussing diabetic carb counting."

Mary-Kate asks, "Diabetic carb counting?"

"Once a month, I have some members teach the others about their illness. Last month was Rachelle and this month is Bray's and MJ's." Nurse Belsh goes over to Rachelle and whispers in her ear. Rachelle nods and Nurse Belsh goes over and opens a door. She pulls out a potluck of different food.

"Bray, MJ, wanna help me pass out the plates and napkins?"

We both get up and start passing it out to everyone. I stumble as I hand a plate to Ty.

"Woah, you okay?" he asks.

"Yeah, I feel a little tired."

"Maybe it's your blood sugar."

"I'm bout to check it in a bit."

"Alright Nurse Belsh! We get to eat some food!" Corey says all hyper, then looks at Rachelle. "Sorry Rache."

"It's okay, Corey."

Man, I wish Rachelle could eat right now. I feel so bad eating in front of her. Her E.O.E is the reason she can't eat.

The doctors don't know what food she's allergic to that caused her to have the E.O.E. Her throat and stomach is inflamed and for some reason, she can no longer eat solid food.

Ty smiles at me. "Right, I been wanting some of your mom's cooking for the longest, Bray."

Everyone gets up to look at all the food.

Nurse Belsh grabs plastic gloves. "Line up so Bray and MJ can put food on yall plates."

Mary-Kate scans the food. "Your mom made this?"

"Yeah, she can cook REAL good, everyone loves her food. I watch her be observant.

"It's true…we all love it." says Ty. "My favorite dish from her mom is the taco salad."

"Me too." Rachelle says.

"I love her spaghetti." MJ says.

Chanel takes a sniff of the food. "Right,"

Nurse Belsh gives us all a squirt of hand sanitizer. "I love her spaghetti too,"

"Her shepherd's pie is my favorite." Kevin says.

I smile at him as I hand him a tray.

"Same, Kevin," says Kayla.

Corey takes a tray from MJ. "Her burgers slap though."

Nurse Belsh hands MJ and I gloves. "We all love her burgers, Corey."

I smile at them. "Thanks guys, I'll let her know."

"You were able to eat it Rachelle?" Mary-Kate asks her.

"Before I stopped eating, I had a lot of Ms. Fletcher's food."

I look at Rachelle and then back at Mary-Kate.

"Well, it looks really good." Mary-Kate smiles shyly.

MJ and I grab spoons and everyone else, except Rachelle, forms a line to the side of the food.

"My mom bought your favorite yogurt, Rache."

"Aw thanks. Is it in the freezer?"

I nod.

"I'll save it for later," she says.

Nurse Belsh tells us to give everyone the same amount using the measuring cups and to pour just a cup of Iced Tea or Mountain Dew. After MJ and I fix our tray we sit down next to each other to start teaching. Nurse Belsh hands Rachelle a big cup of chocolate ice cream.

MJ snaps her finger. "Listen up, kids…"

I shake my head with a smile on my face as everyone gets playfully irritated with MJ.

"So the first food we have is the chicken from 'Captain Jay's'. Chicken doesn't have any carbs because it's meat, but since it has coating-

MJ interrupts. "That's the flour to fry the chicken by the way."

"It has a little bit of carbs." I say, finishing my sentence.

"This chicken isn't a lot…probably like 2 or 3." she says, looking at me for reassurance.

"Yeah," I say. "But something like ten chicken nuggets from Wendy's, it has 15 carbs."

"The next thing we have is the pasta salad." MJ takes a spoonful.

"We got ¼ of a cup and I think it's 10 carbs…it's only the noodles that count. Next is the Hawaiian roll."

MJ eats one. "I love these."

Everyone laughs as I continue.

"I'm actually not going to eat one 'cause I don't like it like that."

Ty takes a bite. "You trippin."

"Leave me alone, okay? I had my mom make it because I know how much you guys love it."

"Anyway," MJ giggles. "The carbs for one is 16...we have 8 fluid ounces of Iced Tea or Mountain Dew."

I take a sip of my tea. "It's 24 carbs."

I'm starting to feel sweaty.

"Then dessert is a chocolate chip cookie." MJ says. "And that's 24 for 2 of them."

"And all together that is," I begin typing it into my calculator that's attached to my purse. "...74 carbs. That's 3 units for me."

MJ takes out her meter. "And I'm gonna take 5 units."

I grab mine out of my purse as we both head to the refrigerator to check our blood sugar so they won't see us.

"Mines low." I raise my meter up, showing MJ my numbers.

"Ooh, 67," she says, worriedly.

Now I know why I stumbled and why I felt hot all of a sudden...great, just great.

I am now starting to feel the rest of the symptoms. I place my pouch back in my purse and go back to my seat.

"You took your shot fast." Rachelle says.

"Didn't need to...my sugar's low.

"Aw, dang." Corey says.

"Wait, how come you can't take the insulin?" Mary-Kate asks. "If you don't mind me asking."

"No, it's fine. Well, when my blood sugar is low, I don't have a lot of sugar and or carbs in me and the insulin turns sugar into energy…so if I'd take it with my sugar being low, the insulin will make my blood sugar go even lower. I need to eat first and if I have to, make the corrections later."

She purses her lips. "Correction?"

"I eat this now because my blood sugar is low but there's only so much I need to eat before the food…well, carbs raise my blood sugar up. So I eat this now and after 15 minutes, I need to check if my blood sugar went up. If it's back to normal, I need to take insulin to cover for the rest of the food."

MJ comes back and starts eating.

"Oh wow." Mary-Kate says.

"Confusing right?" I say.

"Yeah…that's a lot."

I nod with a smile.

"Okay, everyone I got the movie."

Nurse Belsh turns on a documentary about youngsters with diabetes. We all position ourselves to face the flat screen. Ty, moving his chair next to MJ and Kevin next to mine. MJ looks at me and smirks and I roll my eyes at her with a smile on my face. As I watch the documentary, I start to feel dejected.

Watching these stories always puts me in a mood. I always feel this way no matter how many times I've read or seen stories about diabetes…I just wish there was a cure.

I sit back in my chair and think.

Flashback

My mom was confused and angry. "The environment...what do you mean by the environment?"

"Well, I should let you and Bray rest for a little bit. Hopefully her blood sugar will go down and Nurse Nate or Patricia will come back to check it." He headed toward the door.

"What about Raven?" I ask.

He turned back to me. "Or Nurse Raven," he left.

My mom walked over to the window. "I can't believe he just said there's a possibility you got diabetes from the environment and wouldn't even say why he thinks that,"

"Yeah, I caught it too."

"Mm mm mm. Wow, man." she covered her face.

"Mom,"

"Yes sweetie?"

"Am I ever gonna be able to dance again?" I started to cry.

She came over to my side. "I don't know Bray...we can only pray you will."

"I still barely understand what this is."

"I know baby, I barely understand it myself. But trust me you'll get through this, okay?"

I hugged her. "Okay."

She rubbed my back as I began to cry, making her shoulder damp.

I pulled away from her, lying back on the bed. I looked at my fingers, which were bandaged up from the nurses pricking it to check my blood sugar. I closed my eyes as tears rolled down my cheeks and my mom wiped my cheeks.

Flashback Ends

I hug Rachelle goodbye as she leaves to go to her room in the hospital. I turn to see MJ and Ty talking to each other.

Mary-Kate comes up to me. "Hey, Bray…just wanted to say thanks."

I look at her uncertain.

"The food was really great. I haven't had a roll in so long."

"Oh, no problem. I'll let my mom know you thought it was good."

She grins at me and hugs me. At first, I'm shocked but then I hug her back.

She looks at me with sincerity. "I'm so sorry you and MJ have to go through all that,"

"Oh it's okay, we have faith that God will heal us one day."

A soft smile creeps on her face. I am now realizing the small scar under her left eye.

"I know He'll heal you too."

"Yeah."

I grin at her.

She sounds worried as she asks, "Hey do you know anything about the 'story of my life' presentation?"

"Yeah, Nurse Belsh has us to present what actually happened to us when we got our illness, whenever someone new enters the group. Don't worry, everyone did it at one point. We hadn't gotten any new people since I joined 3 years ago though."

"Okay."

"When are you presenting?"

"Next week."

"Don't worry, it's not bad,"

"I'm shy though."

I tilt my head to the side. "It's just gonna be us,"

"Okay."

She pulls her phone out of her pocket as she gets a notification.

"It's my dad...mind if I take a plate home?" she asks.

"Of course, take as many as you'd like," I smile.

"Thanks." she grabs a plate. "This food is so good. Your mom should start a business."

"Yeah, that's what she's been trying to do...I don't know if it'll happen though."

"Don't say that."

"It's just, we don't have the money to start it up."

"You never know. Miracles do happen. Let's talk later. I'll give you my number."

"Yeah, sure."

She gives me her number and I save her contact information.

She starts walking to the door. "I'll see you later."

"See you next Saturday," I wave.

"...see you later Bray." Kevin says while walking towards the door.

"Oh wait,"

He stops and I walk up to him.

"I wanted to ask you if you know when you're having the surgery?"

"It's supposed to be next Monday. Not this Monday coming up and another week."

"Okay, I had wanted to come for support."

"Thanks Bray." He pulls me into a hug.

"No problem."

"See you Saturday." he says, leaving out.

"Okay."

As I'm waiting for MJ, I look to see her talking to Nurse Belsh. As she finishes and goes to the bathroom, Ty and Kayla leave the room saying goodbye to me.

Nurse Belsh begins fixing up the room. "Let your mom know I said thanks again Bray,"

I began helping her. "I will."

"You and MJ still coming tomorrow, right?"

"Yes ma'am." I say.

"Good because I think this is really cool what you guys are trying to do."

Suddenly, the door slams and Nurse Belsh and I jump as MJ runs in.

MJ runs to me pulling my arms and begins spinning me.

Her heavy-handed self...my gosh.

"Bray Bray, Bray, guess what, guess what guess what."

"What girl?"

"Ty asked me out."

"What, really?!"

She squeals. "Yes!"

"What did he say?"

118

"Well, he basically said at the carnival we should hang out together, just the two of us."

"Aww." I smile. "See, he likes you too."

"Ah, finally. Now's the time to show him what MJ is all about." she smirks, while doing a funny pose.

I laugh and say, "I'm so happy for you."

I look at Nurse Belsh and she grins at me.

She begins making herself a plate. "Ty's a really good boy...Who wants the last cookie?"

MJ and I both say together, "I do!"

I look at her sternly. "Half and half then."

She rolls her eyes. "Fine."

We both grab our half and eat it. After a few seconds, MJ checks her phone.

"My mom's here Bray, I'll see you later."

She picks up her things before walking towards the door.

"Okay bye MJ...text me later."

"Alright."

"So how are you doing Bray? How's high school going?"

Nurse Belsh's nurse outfit is so funny and cute. It has little dinosaurs on it. The dinosaurs are trying to eat a banana...so weird...kinda funny? Honestly, it doesn't make sense. I laugh to myself.

"It's good so far I guess. Mostly people from my 8th grade came to the school so it's nice knowing some people."

"Met anyone yet?"

I look at her confused.

"...relationship wise."

"Oh," I smile, "surprisingly I did. We're actually together now. I'm planning on bringing him with me to the carnival." I drink some water.

"Yeah you should. I'd love to meet him. I know your mom is not going to let you just date ANYONE."

"Yeah, you got that right." I say and we both giggle.

Just then my phone starts vibrating. I look at it to see my mom calling. I answer the phone and she tells me she's here.

"Okay Nurse, my mom's here."

"Alright sweetheart. See you tomorrow."

"Okay. Bye." I walk towards the door.

"Bye."

After arriving home, I went straight up to my room to get started working on an essay for English class.

"Research a topic about what you think happens when you die."

The rest I read in my head, already knowing what I am going to put. After 30 minutes I finally finish and I go to my mom's room.

"Hey mom, can I talk to you for a sec?"

I watch as she slides her finger on her phone, not paying attention to what I said.

"Mom..."

"Hm?" she says, still looking at her phone.

"Nurse Belsh said thank you for the food."

"Oh it's no problem."

I grin in relief. "Everyone liked it, the new girl Mary-Kate took a plate home."

"She did?"

"Yeah." I sit on the edge of her bed.

She looks up at me as I do so.

"Are we gonna watch a movie?" I ask.

"Yeah, once Brielle comes back. She went to get something from her house. She should be back soon."

"Okay."

"So I know I asked you last night…but did you enjoy your date?"

"Yes, I enjoyed it a lot. He took me dancing and ya gotta love someone who can dance."

She gives me a half smile.

"No but really, I had fun. He's nice. Different than most boys."

"Okay, then that's good. It's good to know you had a great time."

"Oh I forgot to tell you."

I run to my room to grab the fundraiser flyer and run back to hers.

"Here's the flyer for the fundraiser." I hand it to her.

She takes it and reads it.

"It's next Saturday…do you think we'll be able to go?"

"Yeah, we should be able to."

I lay down on my back. "I was planning on asking Trey if he wanted to come."

"Yeah, that'll be cool." she puts the flyer on her nightstand.

"Okay," I face her. "What time do we have to be at the hospital tomorrow again?"

She picks up her T.V remote and I position myself toward the T.V.

"11:00 a.m."

"Alright. Today at the club, we watched a documentary about people with diabetes."

"Oh." she says.

"Anytime I watch stories like that, it puts me in a mood…and it got me thinking of when I first got diabetes."

She looks down as I continue.

"Do you remember when the doctor had told us I got diabetes…that it was an environmental reason?"

"Yeah but they still don't know for sure how you got it."

"Yeah."

"Ooh this Poppa calling."

I stand up and begin walking towards the door. "Okay. Tell him I said hi."

Before answering it, she says, "Okay,"

I go down the hall to the twins room to find them both doing homework and watching T.V. Their room is so cute. It's basically a room split in half. The walls are painted green and blue but they each have their own decorations and vibes on their side of the room. One huge, flat screen T.V sits in the middle.

I lean against the door. "Math homework?"

They both speak together. "Yeah."

"How was school today?"

They speak together again. "It was good."

That twin telepathy.

"Well I guess later on in the day we're gonna watch a movie."

"Brii not here yet though." Balice says.

"We're waiting for her to get back."

"Oh."

"Until then, do y'all need any help?"

"No thanks."

"Um actually, I do," says Bailey.

I go over to Bailey's bed and help her with her homework. After she finishes, I get under the covers next to her as we watch T.V.

"You guys always watch the same stuff." I grab the remote, trying to find what else is on.

"This is our room." Balice scoffs.

I roll my eyes.

"She is right though, YOU do." Bailey says.

I glance up at Balice as she rolls her eyes.

"Oh look, 'Meet the Browns' is on." I say, getting happy.

As we watch the show, we all laugh hysterically.

I sit up from laughing. "Mr. Brown is so silly."

"I just can't with him," Bailey says, "Look at his pants," she laughs.

I glance back at her giggling. After an hour, I get up from the bed and look outside as I see a white Cadillac Escalade pulling up in front of the house.

She know she fly in that car.

I watch as she walks up to the door. She looks sharp! Her white trench coat and high knee

I move my hand from the blinds. "Brii here."

I go downstairs to greet her as she comes in. After some hours we all gathered in the living room to watch a movie. It was now dusk. My mom and Brielle made cookies and ice cream for us all to eat while watching the movie.

"You talked to Trey today?" asks Mom.

I check my blood sugar. "Yes…we talked a few hours earlier."

I wait for my meter to calculate my blood sugar as Mom bring plates to Bailey and Balice.

217.

I put my meter, pricker, and strips back into my pouch.

Mom walks back into the kitchen. "What is it?"

"217."

She shoots me a 'why-type-of-look' and I shrug.

"I don't know Mom. I guess when I ate earlier, I didn't take enough insulin. Can I just eat one cookie?" I pout.

She looks at me.

"Just one." she grabs her plate and walks out the kitchen.

I open the refrigerator and grab my Lantus pin. I grab a pin needle and twist it on the cap. I then air shot and take my shot in my thigh. I wince as I slowly press the needle into my skin. Pressing the top of pin, I count to 10 and take the needle out. I quickly put my alcohol pad over the spot where a pinch of blood has slowly come out.

I unscrew the needle from the pin. "Well…that hurt."

I get up and throw the needle and alcohol pad away and put my Lantus back in the refrigerator. I grab my cookie and go out into the living room. Irritated, I plop down on the couch next to Bailey and mom. I watch as they all eat their cookies and ice cream.

"Can't even enjoy a night with my fam 'cause of my diabetes." I mumble, hoping no one heard me.

"So what's the new movies we got?" Balice asks.

I grab the white bag on the table and take out the white slips of new movies. The room is dark with only the light shining from the T.V. We all are able to sit comfortably on the long couch and the 2 recliners. Watching movies together is something we all love doing.

"'Molly's Game', 'Mother', 'It', and 'Gifted'.

Brii and mom speak together. "Put on Molly's Game."

"What's that about?" Bailey asks.

"Something about gangs," says Brii.

"Oh." she says.

"Bray, can you look it up?"

I grab my phone and off the table and look up what the movie is about. I explain to them and press play to watch it. After finishing Molly's game, we watched 'Gifted', crying throughout the movie.

"Chris Evans is my boy." I walk up the steps, smiling to myself. "...Well, man." I laugh.

"Goodnight, Bray," Bailey says as Brii picks her up off the stair chair.

"Night…goodnight, Balice and Brii."

They say together, "Goodnight,"

I walk upstairs and into my room and get under the covers quickly. I yawn as I start to think about everything that happened today. I look at my fingers which have bruises and sores at the tips of them.

Dang pricker…

I start to cry a little at the thought of what I have to do everyday. I feel vibration on the bed. I look down to see that it's my phone. I pick it up and read the caller ID.

"Hey Mary-Kate."

"Hey Bray, why are you crying?"

"Um…How'd you know that?" I ask her.

"God just gave me a dream of you crying, so…I figured I'd call."

Woah.

I swallow my spit. "I, I was just crying a bit."

"I know." she giggles, "Tell me what's wrong."

I sigh.

"I was just thinking about my diabetes. I've only had it for three years but it seems like it's been way longer. I honestly don't remember my life before I got it…" I scratch my head, "My blood sugar has been irritating me."

I hear her laugh through the phone which makes me giggle.

I wipe my tears. "I'm a freak."

"We're both freaks. Beautiful freaks. Embrace it. I walk around with an oxygen tank, you think people don't stare? I don't care though, I know how to fleek my eyebrows and do some good eyeshadow and liner." we both laugh.

"Period." I say. "People don't even know I'm a diabetic. I tell them and they become so shocked." I rub my nose. I turn my head towards the door as my mom peaks her head in.

"Hey, who are you talking to?"

I move the phone away and whisper, "Mary-Kate."

126

"Oh, don't be up too long." she yawns and walks away.

I put the phone back to my ear and said, "Hello?"

"I'm here."

"But yeah…"

"…you know my pastor said that 'the life that we live is not just for us but for someone else too', so I think God has us go through things so we can one day get better and help someone else though sometimes people don't get better… but it's more so what they did while suffering. Did they trust God? Did they stay in prayer or did they become mad or depressed and turn to the wrong things? That's what counts."

"I've never thought about it like that."

"People tend to get mad at God when really he's just trying to grow and develop us. Strengthen our faith. Y'know change us…but sometimes you can fall into a bad spot on your own if you continue to live in sin. Like people be so angry at God when you know you weren't supposed to be doing something but blame Him and wonder why you're suffering." she laughs. "Like no sweetie, you did that on your own."

I giggle too. "No one's perfect."

"Not true though…we actually can be perfect. Jesus asked God to give us the same anointing He has. We can be like Jesus and do even more than He did. It's for all people, whoever accepts Him and builds a relationship with Him." I can hear Mary-Kate shuffle around on the bed.

"Woah what? For real?"

"Yeah."

I shake my head in amusement, "Jesus is so generous and caring." I smile.

"The world doesn't deserve Him nor God's love."

"Not one bit but God loves the world so much that He sent His son to save us, we can live life abundantly here on earth." I mentally thank God. "Thank you for calling me, Mary-Kate."

"Of course. I hope I lightened up your night." she giggles. I suddenly hear a little boy's voice asking her who she's talking to.

"It's my friend Bray. You'll meet her soon. Now go back to dad's room…sorry 'bout that."

"That's okay. Tell me about your family."

"They're rich and snobby."

Oop.

"I'm kidding," she laughs. "Not the rich part though."

I laugh and we continue to talk for 3 hours.

Chapter Seven Sunday

"Out of his fullness we have all received grace in
place of grace already given."
John 1:16.

I wake up feeling sunlight on my face. I grab my
phone to check the time. It's 8:48 A.M.

I can sleep a bit longer.

20 minutes later my phone vibrates. I extend my
hand out to grab my phone and I look to see a text from
Trey.

It reads, "Good morning beautiful."

I rub my eyes and smile as I start replying back.

"Morning Trey."

"Just 'Trey' huh? I was preferring hubby,
baby, babe or other things..." he texts with a winking
emoji.

I text him the blank face emoji.

"Cocky much?" I ask.

"Yup." he text, "How'd you sleep last night,
dreams of me I bet."

Well technically. I laugh.

"Lol I had a dream that I was at a party and
something happened."

"What?" he asks.

"I don't know. But you and MJ were there and
you guys were running to me."

"Hm, what do you think it means?"

"Beats me. It was like you guys were scaredly worried." I reply.

"Well hopefully it doesn't mean anything."

"Yeah."

We text more for another 15 minutes and I finally tell him I have to get ready to go to the hospital for a meeting. I get out of bed to go to the bathroom. When I'm finished, I go back inside my room to my closet to pick out some clothes and iron them.

Brii is standing in the doorway. "Hey Bray, where you and Mom going?"

I keep ironing, not looking at her. "We're going to the hospital to discuss how MJ and I are gonna plan our Illness Club."

"Oh." she says.

I hear her move closer to me. I turn around to see Brii lying on my bed.

"How long you staying today?" I ask.

"Well, tomorrow I have to go to school and after that, work."

"I thought you started taking college classes online."

"I am, but you know I have one in-person class too."

"Oh." I start changing into my clothes. "You coming Saturday to the carnival?"

"Yeah, probably so."

As I start doing my hair in my mirror, my phone starts to vibrate.

I need to get my ends clipped.

"Who is it?" I ask Brii.

"MJ."

"Answer it, and put it on speaker, please?"

"Hey Bray." I hear MJ's voice on speaker phone.

"Hey girl."

"You gettin' ready?" she asks.

"Yeah. Almost done actually."

"Alright...but girl, guess what?"

"What?"

"Alex just texted me and said we don't have school tomorrow."

"For real?" I ask.

"Yeah."

"How come?"

"Something about a really important staff meeting."

"Oh wow." I say.

"I know, right? At least we get a four-day weekend."

"Yeah."

"But alright, I'm finna get ready, see you there."

"Okay, see you."

Brii hangs up the phone.

"You might want to go eat a tic tac." says Brii. "breath kind of on ten."

"I just brushed my teeth and you didn't even yet- you know what? Get out." I point to the door.

She walks out and I sniff my breath, smelling nothing but mint.

At the hospital...

The day has finally come! MJ and I can finalize our club meeting with children. We've been filling out different forms for the last 10 minutes in a small room on the 2nd floor. I'm so excited!

We set our pencils down after we finish the forms.

"Okay, so have you guys decided on the color of your wrist bands yet?" Nurse Belsh says.

"Well we chose navy blue, the color of diabetes." says MJ.

"We just went with that since the two of us are diabetics."

"Okay and wristbands is something everyone wears who's a part of the club just so we can identify everyone…. So I know when we talked last time, y'all said Saturdays from 2:00-2:45 P.M. would be great times right?"

"Yes," I say.

"Alright, so you two will be over the junior illness club at the hospital. You'll have your own room with all the supplies you'll need. Also, if an emergency happens, there's going to always be a nurse in the room with you guys to help. And then you know there will be a mini fridge filled with snacks and drinks and their medication. There's a section with arts and crafts, a T.V and laptops." Doctor O'reily says. "Parents do you have any questions?"

"Nope, um, I think everything you said is fine," my mom says.

"How many children will it be?" asks Ms. Reeds.

Doctor O'reily says, "Well, a few parents had already asked about us having a club for the little kids, so I'd say about 5 so far but I'm sure once we tell everyone, a few more will come."

Ms. Reeds nods.

Nurse Belsh asks, "Would you guys like to see the room?"

"Can we?" MJ asks.

"Yeah," says Doctor O'reily.

I mentally scream. I clap my hands together.

MJ and I shoot up as Nurse Belsh leads us to the room, and my mom and MJ's follow. After getting off the elevator to the 5th floor, she leads us to a cute, cozy room. Not too many decorations but I'm sure we will decorate with the group.

I say scan the room. "This is awesome,"

My smile fades as I notice a big space on the wall. "Wait, why is this wall blank?"

"Well, I was going to wait till Saturday to tell everyone but y'all are here now…Down the hall in our room we have the same blank wall. We're going to decorate it, signing our names with paint. You know, making it look cool and stuff." Nurse Belsh states while wiping her glasses.

I smile. "I love it!"

MJ agrees. "Me too." she begins looking through the shelves.

My mom looks around the room.

I ask her, "Mom, what do you think?"

"I like it a lot. I think you and MJ will do a great job handling everything."

"What do you think, Mary?" asks Nurse Belsh.

Ms. Reeds says, "I like it too. It suits you guys."

I look around at the designs and different patterns on the wall.

MJ pulls me into a hug. "This is so cool. I'm so happy."

"I know, right?" I smile at her and she returns a big one.

Nurse Belsh scans her clipboard. "You guys will be starting October 21st."

I nod and watch as MJ's smile fades and she starts to look dizzy.

"You okay?" I ask, worriedly.

"Yeah...I think my sugar's low,"

Ms. Reeds demands, "Check it, MJ."

We both take a seat and MJ pulls her pouch out. With her hands shaking, she checks her sugar and it reads 63. She pulls out a snickers bar and starts eating it immediately.

"Oh MJ, you know I don't like your sugar dropping. You okay?"

I wonder if you 'punish' her when it goes low. Like, unfortunately, we have no control over it.

I roll my eyes. I'm no longer a 'fan' of Ms. Reeds.

"I'm fine, Mom, just getting the symptoms."

"Alright let's go home so you can rest," Ms. Reeds says. "Thanks for showing us the room."

"Oh, no problem."

MJ gets up and I tell her I hope she feels better as she starts to head towards the door. A wheelchair is brought to MJ so she doesn't have to walk.

The distance she has to walk will lower her sugar even more.

My mom and I tell her goodbye and they both wave, disappearing into the hallway.

"Well, thank you, Nurse. I really appreciate you showing us."

"No problem…and you're looking really good Bahati."

"Oh thank you, my head just started hurting out of the blue though."

"Imma go to the bathroom."

I don't want to be a part of their conversation, so I walk out of the room and go down the hall to use the bathroom. As I leave the bathroom, I stand beside the door of the room my mom and Nurse Belsh are in. I take my phone out and get on Snap Chat. After a few seconds, I feel someone's presence near me.

"Hey Bray."

"Hey Kevin, what are you doing here?"

"Well, I'm here with my family to talk about the surgery…"

"Oh."

He smiles. "But I just found out that I don't need it!"

"Wait, what?" I ask, confused.

"I don't need the surgery anymore. I'm not gonna lose my arm…it's like the tumor disappeared."

"Oh my gosh, Kevin!" I pull him into a tight hug. "I'm so happy for you!"

He wraps his arms around me and hugs me tighter. I pull away smiling.

"Thank you," he says. "This was literally a miracle from God…I'm so happy."

"It is! We have to celebrate…are you still going to the carnival?"

"Actually, that's what I wanted to talk to you about."

I look at him confused. "What about it?"

"I wanted to know if um, maybe you wanted to be my date to the carnival?"

My eyes widen and I stare at him. I realize I haven't said anything and I finally speak up.

"Are you serious?"

I don't know what else to say.

"Yeah. I mean…if that's cool with you." he gives me a little smile.

I hate to crush his feelings and I've been waiting for him to say how he feels for the longest and he's never said anything. Now I'm with someone and he asks me.

Great, just great.

I say lowly, "I actually have a boyfriend now."

"Really?"

I watch as his smile drops and he tries to hide the fact that he's hurt.

"Yeah, and I plan on bringing him with me Saturday."

"Oh."

I say to try to lighten the mood. "He's a really great guy, you'll like him a lot,"

"I'm sure I will," he says.

Mom comes out into the hallway. "There you are, Bray. Come on, we're about to go."

"Okay." I look back at Kevin.

"Oh, hey Kevin," my mom says.

"Hey, Ms. Fletcher."

"Didn't expect you to be here."

136

He smiles and looks at me.

"I'll tell you later, mom."

"Alright, we'll see you guys later," Nurse Belsh says.

I wave to the both of them. "Bye."

Kevin's looking right at me. "Bye."

I glance back one more time at Kevin to see him standing there, before turning down the hall to the elevator. When we get home, I tell mom everything that happened with Kevin in the hallway and surprisingly, she isn't shocked that Kevin asked me out.

I glance at her. "Really?"

"Yeah, I always knew Kevin liked you. I know you used to like him too."

"Yeah..." I sigh and look up at the ceiling. "I just didn't want to hurt his feelings, ya know?"

She nods.

"But I'm with Trey and I couldn't be happier...I really like him, more than I liked Kevin actually."

To be honest...

"I like Trey too." she turns the channel on her T.V. "I'm just glad Kevin doesn't have to have surgery now."

I sit up. "Me too...Oh, speaking of Trey...I gotta ask him about Saturday."

"Well, go do that now."

I get off her bed and go down the hall to my room. I sit on my bed by my nightstand and pick my phone up from the charger. I lay down and press Trey's name on my phone. The phone rings and he doesn't answer. I put my phone down and close my eyes as I wait for him to call back. After a minute or two, my phone starts to ring.

"Heyy." I say.

"Hey baby girl. Sorry I missed your phone call."

"It's okay…I wanted to ask you if you're doing anything Saturday?"

"Naw I don't think so, why?"

"I wanted to invite you and your family to come to this fundraiser that's a carnival at the hospital." I say with excitement. "Well it's behind the hospital." I giggle a little bit.

Why am I giggling?

"Oh yeah, sure, I'll ask my mom and see what she says."

"And I was thinking…maybe this could be our second date?" I say.

"Yeah. For sure, baby."

I smile and bite the inside of my lip.

I am snapped out of my thoughts when he asks, "What time will it be Saturday?"

"It's gonna start at 4:00 p.m and end at 10:00 p.m. I'll send you a picture of the flyer."

"Okay. So what time you wanna meet up there?"

"I'll let you know the day of, 'cause I still have to go to the club meeting."

"Alright. I gotta go. I'll text you later tonight and let you know what my mom says."

"Okay. Talk to you later."

"Alright baby girl."

He hangs up the phone and I put my phone back on the charger. I grab my camera and go out to the backyard to take a few pictures of the scenery.

I love photography, I smile, *The sun is shining so bright today.*

After about 20 minutes I come back in to see my mom picking Bailey up from the stair chair.

I sit down on the couch. "Where y'all going?"

"Bailey wants to watch Netflix." my mom says.

"Wanna watch 'The Flash'?" I ask her.

Balice walks down behind them. "Which season?"

"One." says Bailey.

"Okay." says Balice.

I grin as Bailey, Balice, and I start watching our favorite show together.

Chapter Eight The Carnival
09/30

"We loved because he first loved us."
1 John 4:19.

Nurse Belsh takes a seat next to Rachelle. "Okay Mary-Kate, whenever you're ready."

I watch as Mary-Kate looks down and gulps before beginning her presentation.

"Hi. My name is Mary-Kate Daniels and I have thyroid cancer. When I was a young child, I was diagnosed with multiple endocrine neoplasia. I have type 2. It was a really hard time for my parents when I was born because I almost died when I came out of the womb. The doctor said I wasn't breathing, so they ran tests and didn't know what was wrong until a few weeks after I was born. They immediately started treating me. My parents prayed and prayed that I would make it…and I did. My mom used to always tell me a scripture saying, 'She laughs without the fear of the future' and that is what I tell myself every day to keep me going…" she throws her hands up, smiling.

I give her a sad smile as she finishes her sentence.

I feel like crying and being happy at the same time.

She smiles shyly at us. "…But yeah, that's my story."

We all applaud her, and she looks down. I don't know what comes over me but in that moment, I stand up and give her a big hug. She hugs me back with the same intensity.

I whisper to her. "You're the one that's brave."

She pulls away and grins at me.

"I'm so sorry that happened to you." I say.

"It's okay.

Nurse Belsh says, "Thank you, Mary-Kate…Okay guys I have a surprise for you, but first help me with this." She pulls out a tray of paint, plastic wrapping, and shower caps.

Everyone except MJ and I look confused as the two of us smile. After 10 minutes of covering the floor with plastic and putting a plastic poncho and shower cap on, we finally wait for Nurse Belsh to tell us what we're doing.

"So if you haven't noticed, we have a blank wall here that we're going to decorate by signing our names and putting designs and patterns on it."

We all look at the wall and then at each other.

Nurse Belsh raises the paint brushes. "Well, let's get to painting!"

We quickly scurry to get a paint brush and a bucket of paint and start painting. An hour later, and we're finished and we all have a little bit of paint on our faces from playing too much. We take a few steps back to look at it.

I smile. "It looks good, you guys."

"Yeah." everyone else says.

Kayla frowns a little. "I think it's missing one thing, but I don't know what."

"Bray, you're the artistic one. What do you think it needs?" Chanel asks.

Everyone looks at me.

"Hmmm." I think for a second, then, look back at everyone. "Just sign what you are."

I go up and sign 'the art freak' and draw a daisy under my name.

Everyone comes up and signs under their name. Rachelle signs the 'girl (not) next door'. Kevin signs 'the believer'. Chanel signs 'the girl with issues not tissues.' Corey signs 'the attention getter'. Ty signs 'Nothing without twin B'. Kayla signs 'Nothing without twin A." Mary-Kate signs 'miss know it all'. and MJ signs 'the rebel with needles'. We all take a step back and look at our work.

Nurse Belsh puts her hand on my shoulder. "Nice one Bray."

We all hug, fist bump, and high five each other as we smile at our work.

"Okay guys, I gotta take a picture of y'all in front of the wall." Nurse Belsh says, getting her phone out. "Smile!" she snaps the picture.

Back at home, Mom pops in while I'm getting changed.

"How was the club today, Bray?"

"It was awesome, Mom. Today we decorated the wall and it was pretty cool." I change out of my clothes. "What time is it, Mom?" I follow her into her room to grab some lotion.

"3:30."

She's putting Bailey's hair into a ponytail. "Did you tell Trey what time you're gonna be there?"

"Nope, I'm bout to call him now."

I go in my room and pick my phone up to call Trey.
I press the speaker button as the phone rings and I change
into my grey adidas outfit for the carnival.

"Hello."

"Hey Trey."

"Hey, baby girl."

"So we're probably gonna get there around 5:00
p.m."

"Okay. I live a little further from the hospital so it's
gonna take us a little longer to get there, but I'll let my
mom know."

"Alrighty. Well, just call me when you get there."

"Okay."

"K. Bye."

"See you."

I go back inside my mom's room so she can help
me with my hair. An hour has passed and it is now 4:15.
After making sure I have all my medicine and supplies, we
all finally leave the house to go to the fundraiser. We arrive
30 minutes later. We all got out of the car to help my mom
with grabbing Bailey's wheelchair from the trunk. After
Brii lifts Bailey out of the car, we make our way towards
the carnival entrance.

*Ooh, it's so many rides! 'The screamer', the 'freak
out', and a ferris wheel!*

We go in and get our wristbands. Scanning the
crowd, I see the people from the club. They spot me and
come over.

"Hey Bray," says Kevin and Chanel.

"Hey guys." I hug them. "Where's MJ?" I ask.

Chanel points over to a game, and I see MJ and Ty playing and laughing. She soon realizes that Kevin and Chanel are gone, and she comes sprinting to me. She greets and hugs me.

"Hey Ty," I give him a hug.

"Hey shortie," he says, returning it.

They all greet my family.

"Where are you guy's family?" I ask.

A few of them say. "Around here somewhere."

"Already left us alone," Ty says.

I grin and turn my head to the left as I hear a familiar voice. I tell my friends 'I'll be right back' as I head to the voice. I watch as he pushes one of his friends and continues laughing as they get ready to leave from the basketball station.

"Hey peanut."

Chris glances at me before telling his boys he'll catch up.

"Look at you lookin' all cute in that Adidas outfit." he turns his head to the side. "For once in your life."

I scoff as he begins to laugh.

"At least I'm not dressed like Pinocchio. Like for real, what are you wearing?" I look him up and down.

Red knee shorts, big yellow shirt, black sweater, and a yellow bucket hat…my gosh.

"Does MJ know you're here? She'd love to see you." I giggle and he rolls his eyes.

"I don't think so."

"What are you doing here anyway? You usually don't come to these things."

"It's a carnival, Bray."

144

"But it's a fundraiser…you usually don't want anyone to know you're a diabe-

"Because it's no one's business."

"And I get that but you're here with your friends for the first time…just curious." I grin at him.

He glances at his friends before locking eyes with me.

"…I-uh was hoping I'd have the chance to talk to you."

"You sure about that? I don't want your nose getting all long on me."

"Shut up."

I giggle and he laughs.

I'm definitely gonna take a picture of him when he isn't looking.

"I had a dream last night."

I stare at him, "Okay…"

"I dreamt of this boy…I didn't know who he was but the weird part was, you were there watching him and, and you guys started arguing and…um-never mind. Just forget I even said anything."

I pause before saying, "Wait, what…You don't wanna tell me now?"

"Yeah…I'm sorry to have wasted your time…see you at school." he walks off, leaving me confused.

He dreamt that I was watching a boy and begun to argue with him…that's not weird at all.

Then suddenly, my phone starts to vibrate in my purse. I look at my phone to see Trey calling me.

"Hey."

"Hey, I'm here."

"Okay, just come through the entrance and I'll be right there."

"Alright." he says before hanging up the phone.

I run back to my friends and tell my mom that Trey's here.

"Okay, let's go," she says.

I smile and to the club members I say, "There's someone I want you all to meet! Be right back guys."

My family follows me to the entrance of the carnival. I spot Trey in the crowd and see him staring back at me. I look down at his outfit. He's wearing a grey Adidas outfit with a visor to match.

Man, he looks good. A whole snack.

I laugh to myself.

Seeing him come closer makes my stomach fill with butterflies.

I watch his eyes sparkle as we lock eye contact. "Hey."

"Hey." I smile. "So, I see why you wanted me to wear my *'grey'* adidas outfit."

He keeps smiling at me. "I wanted to match." he winks,

and I feel my heart beat out my chest. I snap out of our gaze and finally gather my words together.

Trey is one of those types of people that's too good to be true. Like a main character in the movies.

"Um…guys, this is Trey. Trey, this is my big sister Brielle. My little sisters, Bailey and Balice, and you've already met my mom, Ms. Fletcher."

"Hi," my sisters say.

"Hey, it's nice to meet you guys. This is my mom, Mrs. Williams. My dad, Mr. Williams and this is my little sister, Angela. Dad, this is Bray, my girlfriend."

I turn to look at Trey's dad. He's tall like Trey and looks exactly like him. Same skin tone, same face shape. The only thing is Trey has his mother's eyes. His mother is beautiful and dark skinned.

I smile as Trey's dad looks at me.

"Nice to meet you. You're a very pretty girl, Bray."

"Thank you." I grin. "Hey Mrs. Williams."

"Hey Bray. It's nice to see you again Ms. Fletcher. You have very beautiful girls, Bahati."

"Thank you. You have a handsome son and a beautiful daughter as well."

"Thank you." she says.

I look down at Angela and smile at her.

"You're Bray?" she asks.

"Yes.'

"Trey talks about you all the time."

I laugh. "Oh really?"

"Yes. He says you're the prettiest girl he's ever seen...other than me of course."

We all laugh, except Trey, who blushes a little.

This girl has some sass to her...I like it.

"Okay Angie, that's enough."

"Alright guys, let's get to these rides," my mom says.

"Yes let's get it started!" says Angela.

My mom tells me to call her periodically and I tell her okay. Trey's and my family walk off to get on rides.

"I like your little sister...she's so cute and sassy."

"Yeah, like I said, 8 going on 18."

I laugh as he takes my hand and we start walking. "I have some more people for you to meet."

We walk over to the spot where my friends are. I glance at them to see Mary-Kate and Kayla waiting with them too.

"Hey guys, this is my boyfriend Trey," I say with pride.

Trey smiles. "Hey everyone."

Rachelle blushes. "You are cute!"

Trey laughs and looks at me. They each introduce themselves to him.

"This is Kevin." I say.

"Hey Kevin...Bray's told me a lot about you, about all you guys." Trey says.

"Yeah, same here. It's nice to meet you too." says Kevin.

I look at Kevin and he stares at me.

"Hey MJ." Trey smiles.

"Heyyy."

Ty scoffs.

Oop.

"What?" her head snaps to Ty. "Boy, don't start acting like that, you know I'll cut you off- " she snaps her fingers - "Real quick."

MJ walks away and Ty scurries and follows. I try hiding the fact that I think it's funny but I can't help it.

I laugh. "Did you guys see the look on Ty's face?"

Everyone starts giggling.

"Alright, well, we're about to go on a ride. You guys wanna come?" I ask, finally catching my breath from laughing.

"Yeah, come on." says Corey.

We all scurry off to get in line for the 'Freak Out'. I eagerly wait in line as I watch the ride that sits at least fifteen people, spin around and swing from right to left. After waiting two minutes, we finally get on and we have the best time, laughing and screaming. We went to the carnival this past summer but I always forget the thrill when riding the rides. It catches off guard but it's so fun! After a while of going on many rides and playing games together, Trey and I break off from the group and I get my camera from my mom to take pictures. I take pictures of Trey, my family, and my friends too. He asks to take pictures of me, and I'm a little surprised he knows how to take pictures with a digital camera. When we finish taking pictures and videos, Trey and I go to a basketball carnival game. At first, we're both hitting the same score, but he ends up winning.

"Here's your prize." says the employee.

He gives Trey a blue dog and Trey gives it to me. I smile, looking at the blue dog. "This is so cute."

Trey has a confused smile on his face. "It is, isn't it? I've never seen a blue, stuffed dog."

"What about me Trey?" I turn around to see Angela pouting at Trey.

She appeared out the blue.

"Really, Angie?" Trey says, and she bats her eyelashes.

I giggle and hand her the blue dog. "Here." I say.

"Bray, you don't have to give her that." Trey says, assuring me.

I reassure him. "No, it's okay."

He gives me the 'really' face and I give him the 'it's fine' look.

Angie hugs me unexpectedly. "Thank you, Bray!"

I hug her back and tell her she's welcome.

"Go back to Mom and Dad, Angie," Trey demands.

"Fine. I'm telling Mom you're being mean."

And with that she runs back to her parents.

Trey shakes his head in annoyment. I laugh as he puts his arm around my neck.

"You're-

Trey opens his mouth to say something but stops when we hear a female's voice call my name from a crowd. I turn around to see a chubby girl with glasses and shoulder length, black, and curly hair walking up to me. I smile as she extends her arms out to give me a hug.

I smile. "Hey Alana." I hug her tightly.

"Heyy." she says while hugging me. "How have you been?"

"I'm good. How about you?"

"I'm good." she smiles.

"How's your family?"

"They're great...thanks again for taking my family out to dinner."

"Oh it's no problem. Trey, this is Alana, Alana this is my boyfriend Trey."

"Hi, nice to meet you." Alana grins.

"Hi, and you too." Trey grins.

"Where's your mom?" I ask.

"She didn't feel like coming this time. Where's yours?"

I glance around. "Around here somewhere."

She pulls me over and whispers, "El es lindo."

I laugh and say, "Yo se, verdad."

"Well, I'll let you two go. Nice seeing you, Bray. I missed you a lot, thanks again for helping my mom out. We'll have to hang soon."

"Oh, most definitely Alana, and it's no problem… see you soon."

"Adios."

She walks back to her boyfriend who waves at me before walking off. I wave and Trey and I start walking and he puts his arm around me again.

"She seemed nice."

"Yeah. We look out for each other."

"That's nice…quick question?"

"Yeah?"

"Are you mixed with Hispanic, or no?"

"No, I'm African American. I just grew up in Mexican town."

He side eyes me. "And you know Spanish?"

"Just a little from Spanish class." I say in a 'duh' tone and he laughs which makes my stomach flutter.

"…and uh, about the stuffed dog…"

I smile and look up at him.

"I got something better for you anyway."

I squint my eyes. "And what's that?"

Trey looks up for a second and looks back at me.

"Let's get on the ferris wheel."

"Okay." I say.

And we make our way to the Ferris wheel.

"It's so pretty up here. You can see the moon out already." I glance up at the sky and all the other rides.

Trey looks into my eyes. "I've seen prettier."

I laugh and look away.

"Too cheesy?" he asks.

"YES but it's okay, I like it."

He smiles and gives me a kiss on my forehead.

"What time is it?"

He pulls his phone out. "Uhh, 7:40 P.M." he puts it back in his pocket.

"They'll be playing the movie at 8:00."

"It's kind of chilly up here. You cold?" he asks.

"Yeah, a little."

"Here."

He takes off his blue jean jacket and I thank him, putting it on. As Trey scoots closer to me and cuddles with me, I notice from under his sleeve on his left arm a tattoo showing on his muscle.

 I gasp with a smile on my face. "You have a tattoo?"

I mentally scream.

"Oh, yeah."

He nervously looks down and I smirk at him. "You know we not supposed to have tattoos."

"Yeah...I NOW understand why. I'm not getting another one." He glances at me and shyly smiles.

"When did you get it?"

"In the summer."

"Can I see?"

My focus is taken off of Trey for a second as I realize this dang ride has stopped at the top middle.

Why the heck did they just do that? Ooh, don't rock...please don't rock.

Not bothered by the ride stopping, Trey lifts the left side of his shirt before taking his arm out. He holds the shirt up to his shoulder revealing a tattoo of a beautiful old woman.

"That's a big tattoo. How far does the hair spread?"

"Middle upper part of my chest and a bit on my shoulder and back."

I trace my fingers along the ink. "She's beautiful. Who is she?"

"My grandmother...she passed away last year and I begged my parents to let me get a tattoo of her when I turned 15."

I say with sadness in my voice. "Oh wow, I'm so sorry to hear that Trey."

"It's alright baby girl. Ya know, she was a diabetic too." he wraps his arm back around me, pulling me close.

He takes my hand in his and uses his thumb to slowly caress it.

"She died because of it, but that's how she met my grandfather. They went to high school together and met in the nurse's office."

I look sincerely at him and he continues to play with my hand.

"They really loved each other. They had a kid before getting married and then got married and had another...my mom. And when I was born, they cherished me. Growing up seeing them so in love with each other, I

153

always wanted that. To treat a girl with respect, to spoil her, to tease and play with her...to love her with everything I have, and for her to love me the same way."

He looks down at me and smiles as he says the last part.

"Your nails are so long...you literally change your nail polish every week." he examines my nails and I burst out with laughter. "Don't get me wrong, I like it."

I continue giggling as he kisses the back of my hand. I watch as his smile fades and he looks out into the park.

"I just, I thought it would've been the same with my parents." he mumbles a curse word after.

"What do you mean?" I ask, confused.

He shakes his head and looks down.

"Hey, you can talk to me." I put my other hand on top of his. He glances at me and looks down.

"A few years ago, my dad cheated on my mom and she almost divorced him because of it."

I look at him with my mouth open in shock.

"The only reason she didn't was because Angie was only five, and she didn't want her to grow up without a dad. So she stayed...It's sad. I don't even really go to my dad for advice. I ask my grandpa." he scoffs. "I honestly feel like that as-

The ride suddenly creeks, but not moving in a circular motion yet cutting Trey off and scaring me a bit.

"Okaaaay." I say, worried. "Continue...please,"

"I think he still cheats though, because nowadays all they do is argue...and sometimes, I just wanna take Angie and leave to my grandparents, I mean grandpa's house...but

I know if I leave my mom, he'll hit her, just how he hit me."

"He hit you?!" I hear him curse under his breath.

"Once, when they were arguing. I tried telling him to not yell at mom and he smacked me."

"Oh my gosh, I am so sorry...was this...recently?"

He nods before looking down.

I feel myself starting to get teary eyed. I realize that even though Trey isn't going through something physically like I am, he still is going through something mentally. I would have never thought this was happening to him. I didn't really know what to say from all that except that I'm sorry this is happening to him. He looks at me and smiles sadly.

"The times when we were talking on the phone...?"

"Yeah, they were arguing." he says and clenches his jaw after. "If my parents do end up getting a divorce, I'm going with my mom. The only thing is...my dad is the one that works and if my mom leaves, then we won't have anything...I know my dad loves her and she loves him but sometimes I wish...I don't know." he trails off his sentence and looks up.

"Hey, it's gonna be okay. You just have to be strong for your sister and pray that everything works out for the better with your parents. Hey, look at me..."

He slowly lowers his head and locks eyes with mine.

"It's going to be okay, trust me, you'll get through this. God has you." I smile shyly. "...and I'll be here when you need me."

He smiles at me and continues to look me in my eyes.

"And…I don't even know where my dad is. He hasn't called or text and I think the last time I talked to him, I was probably 8 or 9 and it was through the phone. He has no clue what I'm going through and if I ever did see him, I'd be so angry with him. So I…I guess I know how it feels to not want anything to do with him."

He looks down for a bit, thinking, but I couldn't tell what about.

He chuckles a bit. "I guess we both have messed up dads."

"Yepperdoodles, I guess we do." I give him a half smile and he chuckles again.

"The heck is 'yepperdoodles'?

"My word. Don't go around saying it."

He laughs even more.

"Trust me, I won't." he catches his breath and I giggle as we interlace hands.

"I just wish people wouldn't cheat. At least have the guts to break up with that person first. Now maybe you start to lose interest but cheating really makes you the bad guy. It's just like, don't get in a relationship if you're not gonna commit and be loyal…and I'm not just talking about your parents, I'm talking about every girl or boy, woman or man that thinks it's okay to cheat. And there are no mistakes. I don't care if you're drunk or high or you didn't mean to. When that person has been sticking with you through thick and thin and you break the promise you made by showing love to someone who probably doesn't even care about you? I will never be able to understand why people do that. It makes me want to buy one of those foam, number one hand things that they serve at a game and beat the mes-

I slowly turn my head as I hear Trey chuckle.

"What's so funny?" I ask.

"You are so cute when you rant, and you're absolutely right." he kisses my forehead.

"I know I'm right,"

He laughs. "What did I do to deserve you?"

I smile and take a breath, "Well…I guess I'm just one of a kind."

His face softens. "Yes, you are."

He looks at my eyes and then at my lips and starts to lean in. I do the same until the ride starts to move again, breaking the moment. I move back as we're about to get off the ride.

"Hold on, my mom's calling." I answer the phone.

After finishing the call, I let Trey know that my mom wants me to come to her. She lets me know that they're not staying for the movie, but Trey's mom offers to take me home. My mom is hesitant at first but then says yes. She tells me to make sure I check my blood sugar and eat a snack. After saying goodbye to them, I pick a spot under a weeping willow to watch the movie. I hear someone call my name.

"Bray!" MJ shouts while smiling.

I smile as I see her on a blanket with Ty. She smirks and gives me a sidelong look while Ty is on his phone. I shake my head in amusement. I look to the left of them and see Corey.

I'm so glad Corey decided to come.

157

To the right of Corey, is Rachelle, and Chanel on a blanket together and then next to them, Mary-Kate, and Kevin next to her. I look back to see Kevin looking at me. I smile and wave and he does the same.

"I don't know why you got me under this tree." Trey rolls his eyes. "All these bugs."

"Don't roll your eyes. We'll face the 'fears' of bugs together." I say, dramatically.

I grab my blood sugar pouch and walk to the ice cream stand. I sit on the bench and quickly check my blood sugar. It's 185, so I grab some ice cream on the way back to Trey. Getting ready to watch the movie, I cuddle with Trey having my back against his chest.

"What's your sugar?" Trey asks.

I take a spoonful of my ice cream. "185."

"You sure you're good to eat all that?" he asks, concerned.

Boy, yes. Nothing will stop me from eating ice cream.

"Yeah, they give out yogurt ice cream so that it's less carbs."

"Just making sure."

"Thanks," I say.

"Gimme some."

"Uhh, excuse me? I do NOT share MY ice cream. You better go get your own."

He gives me a blank stare and I return one.

"I'm eating all this. So no, you cannot 'get some'." I try to mock his deep voice. "You must think I'm crazy, giving you some of MY ice cre-

As I'm about to put another scoop in my mouth, Trey quickly puts his mouth on my spoon, eating the ice cream. I gasp out and he starts laughing.

He must be crazy!

"Trey!"

"What?"

"You ate my ice cream...*Don't ever eat a girl's ice cream!*" I whisper at the end while narrowing my eyes.

He starts laughing even more.

"I'm so getting you back for that."

"Mhm. Sure."

"Oh you don't think I will?" I put my ice cream down and sit up on my knees.

"Nah." he says and picks up a spoonful of my Ice cream.

I gasp once again.

"You wanna get down, fizzle brain?" I put my arms out and he side eyes me while slowly chewing the sprinkles.

"First off, don't ever call me a fizzle brain again and second..." He takes his visor off before standing on his knees, so he is a few inches away from my face. He looks down at me and my heart beats faster. He wraps his arms around my neck, hugging me for a second as he gently rocks me side to side. He leans down to my ear.

He whispers, "I don't think you're ready to see what it is to get down with me yet."

I can't help but feel the electricity shoot through me as his breath goes through my ear.

"...umm what are you talk-

I yelp out as Trey gently but quickly tackles me to the ground and he starts to shower me with kisses on my cheeks and forehead which makes me giggle tremendously.

He slides his hands off me before saying, "This is what I meant, Bray. I have morals, baby girl." he gets off me after winking and sits back down on his spot.

I fold my arms. "You sure are different than most boys.

It's what I love most about him...

Woah. Love? No...of course not? That was a 'in the moment' type of saying. Yeppers. I "love" that he's different just how I "love" the fact that the Dolan Twins are "different". Yeppers. They're playful and handsome brothers who have a YouTube channel together...don't see that every day.

"You okay there?" Trey asks, snapping me out of my thoughts.

"Yeppers. Um, where are your parents anyway?"

"With Angie in the car. Now come sit your fine Abby Shoe Shop down," he says assertively and pats the spot in front but between his legs. I blush and sit down in the position we were before. At the last scene of the movie, Trey whispers in my ear.

"I didn't get to give this to you on the Ferris Wheel."

He extends his hand out revealing a medium-sized box.

I smile, confused. "What is this?"

"Open it," he smiles at me.

I giggle. "How the heck were you able to keep this on you while being on the rides?"

I eagerly remove the top of the box, revealing a gold necklace that has a gold flower with a silver diamond in the middle of it.

"Knowing you love floral and seeing as you wear something floral every day to school...I figured you'd want another accessory." he chuckles a bit.

"I love it, this is so amazing Trey."

Trey's eyes light up through the dark as he smiles at me.

"Thank you!"

He kisses the back of my hand and I blush. "You're welcome...I have a question, though." he positions himself a bit so he could face me more. "Why do you love flowers so much?"

"Well...because...I think of it like this. How can something so delicate and beautiful grow in this cold, cruel world? Kind of like what Tupac said, I believe that flowers do grow from concrete. Even though people made this world so ugly...metaphorically speaking...there are still beautiful things in it. To me, it represents one of the beautiful things that God put into this world to let us all know that even though you go through different things, through God, there's always gonna be something, someone or someplace to make it turn out right. For me, it's the flower."

"Wow...that was so beautiful...and deep."

I laugh and look at my necklace.

He asks, "You like poetry?"

I nod and he cuddles up with me again. "You should write."

"I should, shouldn't I?" I say, sarcastically.

"Yeppers." he laughs.

I gasp. "Do not steal my word!" I say, sternly and he rolls his eyes while laughing. Hearing him laugh makes me relax.

Gosh, I love his laugh.

I smile and continue to look at him as he focuses his attention back to the movie.

Everything about him is perfect. His personality, I giggle to myself.

His laugh, his eyes. Oh, his eyes.

I gush thinking about them.

They're like looking into an emerald with chocolate inside it. His hair...his whole face is just attractive...and his lips...

He notices me staring at him and cracks a smile.

With his eyes still on the screen he asks, "What?"

"These last few weeks have been some of the best weeks of my entire life...so far." I mumble the last part.

He looks down at me.

"I'm so glad that I met you."

He licks his lips and smiles widely, which makes my heart skip a beat.

"Man," he chuckles to himself, "If only we weren't in public right now."

I nervously laugh and look away from him.

"Oh, I don't mean it like that, Bray." he reassures me. "Who's the perverted one now?"

I laugh.

"I just mean if we weren't in public right now, I'd probably be doing flips off the wall. Yep. I like you that much and I'm not afraid to admit it."

Oh my gosh this boy is so cheesy.

He looks at me and bites his lip. "I'm glad I met you too. I've never met a girl like you...you're...you're special, Bray."

I smile and look him in his eyes. Trey cups my face with his right hand and traces my bottom lip with his thumb. The movie ends and as Trey slowly leans closer to me, fireworks go off in the sky. In that moment, I feel my breathing increase and my heart beats faster as he kisses me slowly and sweetly. I hear people clap as more and more fireworks are set off but the only think my focus is on is Trey. We slowly pull away and put our foreheads together.

"You're pretty good," he says.

I start laughing and he chuckles with me.

"This is not gonna be something we do often, okay?"

He smiles and says, "I know..."

I smile back and look away from him.

After a few seconds, I feel his hand on my face again and I look back up at him. He slowly pecks my lips once more. We pull away and everything around us fades away and it's as if we are the only people there. I'm no longer paying attention to the fireworks. We keep looking at each other because we both knew watching the fireworks wouldn't compare to what we feel when we look at each other. Out of nowhere I feel someone slide by me, nudging me. I turn my head to see MJ.

"And that is the ending of our Annual Lakeside Fundraiser, everyone. Thank you all for coming and have goodnight! Enjoy some music on your way out!" a man with a microphone states.

MJ pulls me to my feet and screams out as the fireworks continue to go off. I scream out with her and all my friends come over and scream too. Trey stands up and laughs and I look around to see all the people from the hospital screaming, clapping, yelling, and laughing as music starts playing. Soon enough, all the teens and children dance all around the field. I look around to see kids in wheelchairs and walkers laughing, people with different illnesses that I've met were laughing and having fun. Trey picks me up and spins me around.

Chapter Nine Friendship
10/07

"Carry each other's burdens, and in this way, you
will fulfill the law of Christ."
Galatians 6:2

Flashback

A year ago at Lakeside Hospital 9:45 p.m

Rachelle yawned. "Okay this movie is boring."
I adjusted myself on her hospital bed.
"Rachelle...we're only 10 minutes in! Never judge a movie
until you finish the whole thing." she laughed while
reaching out to grab her yogurt.
"How's the Greek yogurt?"
"It's good..." she took a spoonful. "I just wish I
could have actual food...solid food."
"I know," I said softly, "You will soon."
I looked over to Rachelle as she put her head down
and began to cry. I sat there and looked down. She sighed
heavily.
"I just, I just don't understand why I can't eat solid
food. It's like my esophagus is infected or something. And
I'm still losing weight, Bray. Every week."
I began to cry with her.

"I'm so weak, Bray. I literally have no strength in me and I'm SO hungry. And I don't have a butt anymore!" she cracked a laugh and I did the same.

She wiped her tears. "I mean, I'm flat as that lady that works at Old Navy!" she sniffed and ate another spoonful.

I cracked up and pulled her to me.

"Eosinophilic Esophagitis!" she shouted.

"You will get better soon. No matter how it may look, God is listening to you and He sees you. God sent all these doctors to help you get better."

"Why did I get E.O.E?"

I smiled. "Why did I get diabetes? God will tell us someday."

She looked down. "Yeah…" After a few seconds, she says, Thanks Bray, you're a good friend."

She playfully slapped my face.

"Okay, okay, ow." I moved my arm from around her.

"Love you," she said.

"Love you too."

Flashback Ends

"So Bray, are you still going to homecoming?"

"Yeah, Trey and I talked about it last week," I take a bite into my breakfast sandwich. "He already paid for my ticket."

Another Saturday has come. Homecoming is literally next week! I never thought I'd be going with a date for my first homecoming! So much has happened in the last four weeks.

"Okay then." Brii says. "In that case, we're going dress shopping after the club meeting."

"I'm sorry for the short notice, considering it's only a week from homecoming," I say.

"It's alright. I had picked 4 dresses that I thought you'd like just in case and I put it on hold for you."

I get up and give her a hug. "Aw, thanks Brielle."

She smells like strawberries.

"You're welcome. Once you pick your dress, you'll get your hair and makeup done the day of."

"Why not the day before for my hair?"

"Cause Ranita won't have any openings until then. But you gotta be there at eight in the morning."

"Oohkay."

"You'll be getting your eyebrows and nails done that Friday."

After finishing my breakfast, I go upstairs and grab my purse, phone, and charger.

"I'll bring my camera," I grab it and go back downstairs.

"You ready, Bray?" my mom asks, grabbing her purse.

Mom has on a purple, sweater dress with her hair in a bun. She even has some makeup on…she looks like grandma. My grandma passed away when I was 3 months old…I don't remember her but Mom tells us stories of her whenever she can. Her favorite color was purple. She was a singer, so she loved listening to many songs. She loved shopping and many other things…I got my middle name from my great grandma. Clara.

I smile to myself.

"Yeah, I'm ready…let me grab a sweater."

She grabs her keys. "What was your sugar?"

"Well earlier it was 200 and when I just ate it was 216."

"You took insulin?"

"Dang nope," I rushed back into the kitchen.

Do not need my blood sugar going high…how could I forget taking it?

I quickly take my Apidra pin out and grab a needle to take my shot.

To myself, I say, "2 pieces of bread is 26, 1 cup of sunny D is 28, so 54 is 3 units."

I turn the scale on the insulin pin to two and press the top so the air can come out. I take the shot in my arm after turning it to four. I hurry and put it back in the refrigerator.

"I'm good." I head towards the front door.

I watch as my mom gives me the 'really' stare and she follows behind and yells to everyone she'll be back.

At the hospital…

"So are you taking Ty to homecoming with you?" I ask, smirking.

MJ smiles. "Yeah…I was able to get a guest ticket for him just before they ran out."

I squeal. "Yay, our first double date!"

MJ suddenly looks worried. "I need help picking out a dress, Bray,"

"I'm going today to get mine. I'm sure mom wouldn't mind if you came along."

"Really? I'll bring my own money; it's just my mom won't have time to take me shopping for a dress."

"Yeah. We'll have them talk when the meeting's over."

She hugs me. "Okay."

Nurse Belsh enters the room. "So I was just informed that homecoming for 4 of you is next week, so there will be no meeting next Saturday...Kevin's school, Corey's school, and Bray and MJ's school."

"I'm not planning on going anymore anyway." Kevin says.

I look back at him and he glances at me.

Corey shrugs. "I never go, so..."

"Aw why not?" I say.

In a harsh tone, he says, "You know why." I frown and look away.

Gosh.

He clears his throat and quietly but quickly apologizes. "I don't want everyone staring at me."

"I'm sorry," I say. "All I'm saying is people will stare at how good you'll look in a tux." he grins.

"You better walk in there with some pride." I encourage him. "See? Like this."

I get up and do a serious walk. I look at him to see him cracking up. He shoots me a big smile.

"Thanks, Bray."

I grin and sit back down.

Nurse Belsh says, "Give me one second, I have to grab something from the front desk." she leaves the room and I hear laughter. I look behind me noticing Mary-Kate and Kevin talking and laughing with each other.

Mary-Kate looks so pretty. Her hair is curled and she is wearing makeup. Our relationship has grown a lot. She's so sweet...kind of like Kevin.

Rachelle notices me looking at them. "You okay Bray?"

"Yeah, I'm fine...why'd you ask?"

"Just making sure."

I give her a half smile and she returns one.

"Hey Bray, can I talk to you?" Kevin asks, who is suddenly right behind me.

"Yeah."

We get up and walk over to the back of the room by a window. I noticed a cross chain around his neck.

"Wassup?" I ask.

"Just wanted to say...Trey seemed like a cool guy."

I smile softly. "Well I'm glad you think so."

"Just know I'll always be here whenever you need someone to talk to."

"Thanks Kev."

He smiles and compliments me on my necklace and asks if it's new.

"Yeah, a gift from him."

He chuckles a bit. "He knows your obsession for floral."

I blush, thinking of Trey. "Yeah...he does."

"And I hope he makes you happy." he smiles. "You deserve to be. You're a brave girl."

170

"Thank you," I say, uncertain, with a smile on my face.

Ever since Trey told me I was brave and said that people will start telling me...they have been.

"You deserve to be happy too." I glance at Mary-Kate and smile. "You like her?"

He hunches his shoulders. "I don't know."

He bites his lip and stares at the floor.

"Oh come on, you know if you like her or not."

He smiles and looks up at me. I smile as I look into his sapphire eyes.

"There's one thing I am sure about," he says.

"And what's that?"

"I'll always love you, Bray,"

My mouth is slightly open.

He-he loves me?

"I'm sorry it took me so long to tell you how I felt ever since that day. I was scared then and now I'm not."

I give him a sad smile and he pulls me into a tight hug. We pull away looking at each other for a few seconds. He gives me a kiss on the cheek before he goes back to his seat. I still stand there, shocked at what just happened.

Flashback

Two years ago Lakeside Hospital 8 P.M

I sat on the bean-bag chair, shifting my weight. I was nervous and curious to know what question Kevin was going to ask next.

He tilted his head to the side. "Have you ever gotten into a fight?"

I rolled my eyes. "Noppers! You?"

"Once…I was holding my own for the first few minutes but ended up getting my butt kicked."

I giggled. "Who were you fighting?"

After a few seconds, he looked away from me and said, "My older brother…" We both laughed.

I said, "That does not count as a REAL fight. Siblings fight all the time."

"Guess you're right…your turn."

"Um…ever had a girlfriend?"

"Naw…"

I tilted my head to the side and he looked at me.

"Had your first kiss yet?" he asked.

I began to blush. "No…" I looked down.

"Me either."

Okay…kinda awkward now…a girl who likes a boy, doesn't know if he likes her, are both sitting in a room alone together…movie scene activated.

I glanced at Kevin to see him looking at me.

"Um…wanna head back outside? Unless you have some more questions…"

"No, we-we can head out."

I nodded and we both stood up. I turned to leave.

"Bray?"

I looked back at him. "Hm?"

After a few seconds, he quickly pecked my lips and I stood there in shock.

Oh my gosh. My first kiss…Mom's gonna kill me… But…does he like me? I want to hear him say it.

"Why'd you do that?"

He paused. "I don't know…"

Not the answer I hoped for.

He looked nervous. "You look really pretty right now and…"

Suddenly, Ty comes into the dark-room and leans against the door.

He said, "Come on, the movie's about to start -wait, what y'all doin'…in here?" he squinted his eyes at us while smirking.

We both said, "Nothing."

He slowly left. Kevin and I lightly smiled at each other before leaving the room too.

Flashback Ends

At the Mall…

We've been at the mall for at least 30 minutes. One, we had to find a parking space, which took 10 minutes. Then, walking to the store took another 10 minutes. It's so crowded today.

"Here are the dresses, Bray. Go try them on." Brii hands them to me. I go inside the dressing room, taking the dresses with me. I start to change out of my clothes and I can hear my family and MJ talking.

"MJ, you found a dress yet?" my mom asks.

"I have these two here that I like…but I'm not sure."

"Go change into them, too. So we can all see."

"Okay."

I can hear MJ going into the dressing stall next to mine. After MJ and I try on our dresses, we finally pick the ones we like most. We look for shoes to match and Brii pays for them, not having to pay a lot since she works at the store. Discounts galore.

"Thanks again, Brii. Thanks, Ms. Fletcher. I really appreciate you helping," MJ says.

I give them both a kiss on the cheek. "Yeah, thanks guys,"

"Oh, it's no problem." my mom says.

"You're welcome." Brii says.

We leave the store and drive home to my house. MJ and I go up to my room.

MJ lays flat on my bed. "I can't believe we're about to go to our first homecoming Saturday."

"I know, right?" I lay down next to her. "It seems like it was just yesterday when we met at camp. Like I never knew there was such a thing as diabetic camp."

She looks over at me and smiles.

"I remember when we met Aujanae, Tristian, -

"Hey, Tristian was bae, okay?" we both laugh. "Remember Maya?"

"Yes girl, she was so boy crazy."

"Haha, yeah," I smile, "But she was so nice and crazy in a good way."

"I remember Gabby, and Sydney, and Raegan, and…what's the other girl's name?"

"I don't know, I forgot," I giggle, sitting up. "Was it Francesca?"

"Oh yeah, it sholl was!" MJ says, laughing hysterically. "I miss them."

174

"Me too. You guys were one of the first people I met with diabetes when I first got it."

MJ smiles shyly as she sits up on the bed.

"I wouldn't mind going back to Camp Midicha...but I think we're too old now.

"I thought it goes up until we're 16."

"Probably so...I could use a few days to just relax and get away from everything. I know we just started school but it's like...it's just too much for me right now. Especially at this school, since they're putting so much pressure on us."

"Yeah...I feel the same way." I lean back on my pillows. "At least we don't have to wear uniforms."

"I was finna say that," she giggles. Then her smile fades. "I think things are getting better with my mom."

I smile shyly and tell her that's good.

"I think she's finally gonna dump her boyfriend, which I'm glad about because he's a bad influence on her. Always having her out late, barely getting any sleep knowing she has to work in the morning...and if that's not bad enough, she's drinking a lot more." She sighs in frustration as she takes her hair out of a ponytail and takes her glasses off.

I say, "I'm so sorry that's happening, if she is gonna break up with him, then it's a good thing."

"Yeah...I just hope someone finds my mom who's gonna love her for her."

I nod in agreement.

"Just how Trey loves you."

She gets up and opens the sliding door to my patio, walking outside.

I get off the bed and follow her. "Oh really?"

She leans over the balcony and glances at me. I look out at my backyard, feeling the cool breeze.

She smiles. "And you finally had your first make out at the carnival."

"I would not call it a make." I say, "And you've brought it up every day since then!"

She chuckles a bit, teasing me. "2017 has been an eventful year. How would you say the kiss was?" MJ pokes at me.

"Good, I guess. It was great…I don't know MJ." I laugh, brushing it off.

She was quiet for a second. "How'd you know what to do? I mean, I know your first little peck on the lips was you know who…"

I glance at her before looking back at the sky. "I…I don't know, I just did…but…kissing him on the lips, it's not something I wanna keep doing all the time, you know?"

She nods. "Yeah, of course…we're only 14."

I nod and she pauses before saying, "I saw you guys at the carnival last week, but it was literally like the song…Bray and Trey sitting by a tree. K-I-S-S-I-N-G. First comes love, then comes marriage, then comes a girl in a baby carriage." she laughs and I cover my ears with a smile on my face.

"Would you shut up?" I grab a pillow and hit her with it. She laughs so hard she starts farting. "Oh my gosh, get your nasty butt out of my room."

I playfully push her and she grabs hold of me making us both fall onto the blue rug in front of my bed.

176

We both start laughing as we put our feet on top of the bed. MJ finally catches her breath.

"I'm serious, Bray...I see the way he looks at you. It's love."

I look up at the ceiling. "I don't know...I know I do have strong feelings for him." I smile, then ask, "Do you think it's possible to fall for someone you haven't known long?"

"I think it's possible, according to all those movies you love to watch."

I shrug. "I mean, it's just the little things you fall in love with."

"Are you falling for him?" MJ asks.

I nod and she smiles.

"See? I told you he was different."

"Well, he definitely changed my mind about love. Not that I didn't believe in it but I thought I wouldn't be able to have it."

"I know. For so long we both agreed we should just get with people who have an illness. At least then, we'd be able to relate to each other."

"Yeah...I guess things have changed. Especially after-"

"Y'all's make-out session?" she laughs.

"No! Oh my gosh, will you stop with that." I try to hold in my laughter but can't. "After this one day last week. I think it was Tuesday after school. We were in the outside part of the cafeteria."

"Were you even supposed to be out there?"

"No, and I was worried we'd get caught but he assured me we were fine." I smile to myself, "I forgot what we were talking about at first but I remember one thing."

Flashback

"You don't think you're beautiful?" he asked.

"No, I do. It's just, sometimes I have to remind myself."

I bit the inside of my lip and looked down. I shivered as the wind hit my face.

The wind's blowing too hard.

Trey took out his phone and began typing something.

I peeked at his phone. "What are you typing?"

"Something I've been working on...I want to read it to you."

I rested my head on my hand as he began. "The ground is heavily wet with cloud's tears and yet my mood remains elated. This world is consumed with unfortunate events and yet when I see her, she is the luck I've needed. The luck the world needs. One smile from her could put any guy at their knees. I, for one, can't bear the thought of giving her up. So I won't. With all the mischief in the world, how can one's presence be so pure and reassuring. Reassuring that there is still good left here on earth. As if the ground she walks on is quite different from everyone else's. So heaven sent that even angels stop and stare. I stare. I try to remember every detail of her. I want to know her if it's the last thing I do. Am I ready to be vulnerable? Will she accept me? I have nothing to offer but a knowledge of knowing morals from Christ. God, she's beautiful. Inside and out. I pray she knows that. Every day I pray for her…" he stopped reading. "That's what I have so far." he looked down.

After a few seconds, I said an outburst. "Um what the heck, Trey?! That was amazing! How are you so…like…I don't even know. Like wow- I can't with you."

He looked at me shyly and I playfully smacked his arm and he yelped out. I put my hands over my face.

"I wonder who you were talking about…" My words were muffled through my hands.

I felt Trey move my hands from my face. He cupped my face with his warm hands and caressed my cheek. He continued to look in my eyes while I looked at his now green eyes from the sunlight. I could still see the brown in them. He softly smiled and kissed my forehead.

"God made you the way you are. Always tell yourself you're beautiful because, because he thought so first…and you're the most beautiful girl I've ever seen…obviously."

Flashback Ends

I smile remembering that day. *In the poem he said he prays for me. When someone takes the time out to pray for you, that shows they really care. You were on their mind that much.*

"What about you and Ty?" I ask.

"What about us?"

"Us?" I tease her. "Well, he seemed to be all over you at the carnival."

179

"Yeah, so?"

"Are you guys gonna make it official?"

MJ shrugs. "I'm just glad he wants to go to homecoming with me. Maybe he'll ask me there."

"Yeah. I hope so and then we'll both have boyfriends."

She laughs and agrees.

"Can you believe we're about to go to our first homecoming, MJ?"

"I know I can! Get ready to turn up for real."

"Right!" I laugh.

We both get up off the floor and I close the door to my balcony. I sit down on my bed.

She starts shaking her butt, dancing silly. "Gotta make sure we look good twerking."

"Oh my gosh MJ." I laugh at her, "You really can't dance."

"Come on girl, shake what your momma gave ya."

MJ pulls me off the bed and slaps me on the butt. I yelp out and hold my butt as she continues to dance. She grabs her phone and turns on music and starts dancing.

"Come on, let's practice."

"Girl. Ain't nobody gonna be twerking on no one doing THAT with anyone." I squint my eyes at her.

"I know." she spins while shaking her butt. "Party pooper."

"Am not."

"Are too."

"Am not."

"Are too."

I slap her with one of my pillows. "Am. Not."

She gasps as she falls to the ground.

"Oh. No. You. Didn't!"

"Oh. Yes. I. Did!"

She scurries and grabs a pillow from my bed and we each get ready to hit each other with a pillow.

"It's on like Donkey Kong with your Mary Poppins lookin' bu-"

"Don't finish that sentence! And what's wrong with my Mary Poppins shirt?" I ask, getting out of my stance.

"Oh, nothing." she quickly wacks me with a pillow and I fall to the ground.

From downstairs, Mom yells, "WHAT WAS THAT?"

"NOTHING MOM, JUST PLAYING."

I quickly got up to see MJ standing on my bed.

"Who do you think you are, standing on MY bed?"

"Rocky."

"Yeah, not with them feet."

She looks down and I smack her legs with the pillow, making her flop on the bed. We continue to pillow fight for another few minutes until we get tired and give up.

I do a victory dance. "Ha, I won."

"Barely. I let you win."

"Like heck you did."

She throws the pillow at me and I throw it back at her. We both laugh as we start dancing to the music. After what seems like forever, we stop dancing and I lay down on my bed.

"So I've been thinking…"

"About what?" I ask.

"For our club, we should have the kids introduce themselves and then do a little dancing game after, or arts and crafts. Have them make a name tag 'cause you know I'm bad at names."

"Ha, there's no doubt there."

She glares at me with a smile still on her face.

"But I agree with you. I am so excited; I can't wait to start." I smile.

"Yeah. Me too." she says.

"I gotta tell you about this weird dream I keep having."

"What was it?" she begins looking for a book on my bookshelf.

"Well, I remember me, you, and Trey being at a party and something bad happens…"

"Like what?" she stops looking for a book and looks at me.

"I don't know. I just remember seeing you and Trey like scaredly worried."

"Hmm," she begins searching for a book again.

"I told my mom about it but she didn't have too much to say."

"What do you think it means?"

"Beats me…I just don't understand why I keep dreaming of it. You guys are looking at me scared before I wake up and it's like you guys were running towards me."

"Hm…well I hope it doesn't mean anything. You know you get really special dreams, anyway. Maybe it's God telling you something."

"Maybe. Mary-Kate and I talked about it the other day."

"You guys are getting close."

I shrug. "We just have a lot in common. She's such a cool person."

"Well I wouldn't know, but I'll take your word for it. Imma borrow this book, okay?" she grabs the book off the shelf.

"Alright."

She walks back to my bed and starts reading the back of the book.

MJ asks, "Where'd you get this book from?"

"Mr. Mathews bought it for me back in 8th grade."

"He bought it for you? Why?"

"Cause I was one of the students to read the most in the class. He bought it for other students too."

MJ flipped open the inside cover. "Aw, he even left this cute little note."

"Yeah, It was nice of him."

"Yeah."

I pick up my phone. "So it's okay if you spend the night still?"

"Yeah, my mom said it's okay."

"Okay."

She puts the book back. "I'll read it when I go home. Let's watch some T.V." she turns it on.

"Okay and Imma ask my mom to make some funnel cakes. Do you want some?"

"Girl you KNOW I want some."

I laugh. "Alright, I'll be right back."

After eating our funnel cakes and taking our Lantus, we FaceTime everyone from the club and Trey. After saying goodnight to them, MJ and I stay up until 3:00 A.M before going to bed.

Chapter Ten Homecoming
10/14

"We can rejoice too, when we run into problems and trials, for we know that they help us develop endurance. And endurance develops strength of character and character strengthens our confident hope of salvation And this hope will not lead to disappointment. For we know how dearly God loves us because he has given us the Holy Spirit to fill our hearts with his love."

Romans 3:5.

"Bray, wake up…Bray."

"Hm?"

"Come on, wake up, you gotta get your hair done for homecoming."

"Oh really…" I say in a sarcastic tone.

"Yeppers," my mom says.

I open one of my eyes to see her smiling.

"Don't use my word."

She laughs and playfully shoves me. I grab her arm and hold on.

She playfully says, "Don't touch me."

I laugh as she starts to tickle me.

She leaves the room while saying, "Come on Bray, gotta get up,"

I yawn and scratch my hair. "Okay…"

I get up and make my way towards the bathroom to get ready.

An hour later…

"Bray, you got all your supplies?" my mom asks.

I put my sweater on. "Yes."

"Alright guys, Bray's gotta get her hair and makeup done so we'll be back in a few hours. Be ready so y'all can take pics with Bray later."

"Okay, Ma." Brii says to her.

"See y'all when we get back."

"Love you." I close the door.

We drive to Ranita's house for an hour and a half. She greets us as we enter her house and I sit down in her salon chair which is in her basement. After a few minutes she gets started on my hair. Two and a half hours later, she finally gets done with my hair.

Ranita takes the cover up off of me. "Okay Bray, go have a look."

I get out the chair and walk to the mirror hanging on the door.

I smile at my hair. "I love the curls."

I turn my head to see pretty rose gold pins.

"It's so pretty…thank you so much."

She smiles at me. "You're welcome, Bray."

"I love it Bray, it fits your little head."

"Thank you, Mom. What time is it?" I ask to go to the bathroom.

"10:47." she yells to me.

I use the bathroom and take a few pictures of my hair before leaving out.

"You ready Bray?" my mom asks, before handing me my purse.

"Yes…thanks again Mrs. G."

"Your welcome, Bray…I'm glad you like it."

I smile widely. "I do."

The three of us walk upstairs to go out the door.

"Okay. Bye Jamie, bye Sophe, bye Mrs. G."

"See you guys." They all say.

"Bye Nita, I'll call you." Mom says before getting into the car.

"Okay." she says.

"Bye you guys." Jamie yells out.

"Bye." we both say.

"Thanks again," I yell out.

"No problem."

I shut the door and we make our way to M.A.C to get my makeup done. After being there for almost three hours, we make our way home, so I can get ready.

"What time is it, Bray?"

"3:30."

"What time did Trey say he'll be here to get you?" Mom asks.

"I told him 7:00 'cause I wanted to go somewhere and take some pictures."

"What time does the thing start?"

"7:30."

"Okay 'cause you don't have to arrive at the exact time…What you want to eat?" she asks.

"How about some Armando's?" I ask, getting happy.

Another favorite Mexican restaurant of mine.

"Okay."

After going to Armando's and getting our food, we go home and eat and I start getting ready for homecoming.

"What time is it?" asks mom.

"5:34." Brii says while giving me my earrings.

"You look good, girl."

"Thank you," I smile. "MJ sent me a picture of her makeup. She looks gorgeous."

"Did you send her one too?" Balice asks.

"No, just wait until you see her," Brii remarks.

"Okay."

I go over and look at myself in the mirror. I smile as I spin around and look myself up and down. A rose-gold dress. Knee length and sleeveless. The material along the top is so detailed and pretty. Plus, I have a rose-gold sequin jacket.

"Thank you, guys, for helping me." I look at my nails and up at them.

"Your dress, makeup, and nails all match," Brii says.

"Yeah." I say.

"Here's your shoes, Bray."

I thank mom and put my shoes on.

Bailey smiles at me. "You look beautiful Bray."

"Thanks, Bailey."

After a while it was finally almost time for Trey to come so we could leave.

"He just texted me and said he's on his way."

"Okay. What's your blood sugar?"

"It was 223."

Mom begins to fix my dress. "Got your strips, meter, pricker, needles..."

"Yes. I made sure it could fit in this little purse."

"Ice pack and insulin?"

"Yes."

"You look so gorgeous, Bray. Come on, let's get a few pictures of you and your sisters."

"Okay."

After taking some pictures of my sisters and I. We hear a knock on the door.

"Must be Trey..." I say, getting happy.

I'm nervous now. I mentally scream.

"Are you gonna open the door or do you want me to?"

"I'll open it." I walk over to the door.

I open the door and smile widely. Trey looks me up and down and smiles widely too.

He locks eyes with me. "Wow, you look breathtaking."

"Thank you, you look very handsome."

"Thank you." he looks down. "I got this for you." he pulls out a plastic box from behind his back.

He opens it, revealing a beautiful rose gold corsage.

"It's beautiful...thank you."

He smiles, takes my hand, and puts it on my wrist.

"Hey, Ms. Fletcher. Hey, girls."

They speak together. "Hey, Trey,"

"You look really nice," my mom says.

"Thank you." he smiles shyly. "You have a really nice home."

"Thank you, sir."

"Are you ready to go?"

"Yeah, you ready mom?" I look back at her.

"Yes. Alright girls, I'm gonna go with Trey's mom to drop them off."

"Okay," they say.

I go over and give my sisters a hug before leaving out the door and walking to Trey's car.

My mom looks out the window. "It's sprinkling outside."

"Do you guys have an umbrella?" I ask.

"Yeah, right here."

Before arriving at homecoming, Trey's mom drives us to Belle Isle to take some pictures. We hug under the umbrella as she takes picture after picture.

Gotta have my photos.

After taking many, she drops us off at Cobo hall.

Trey holds the door open for me and I get out of the car.

"Thanks again Mrs. Williams."

"No problem. You look beautiful, Bray."

"Thank you. I love you, Mom, I'll call you in a little bit."

"Okay sweetie, love you too." she gives me a side kiss on the cheek. "Have fun you guys."

"Thanks, Ms. Fletcher." Trey says.

"Bye, Mom." I wave.

"Bye."

I take Trey's hand as we go inside. Looking around I wave to some of my friends and Trey bro hugs some of his.

"Got your ticket out?"

I show him. "Yeppers."

We give the lady at the front our ID's and tickets, and she tears a piece from the bottom and gives the ticket back to us. She tells us to enjoy our night and we walk in. I look around to see a huge crowd gathered in the giant room.

Everything looks green. I guess they have a green lighting effect in this room.

"Let's find a table."

"Okay."

Still holding hands, we squeeze through people and greet people that we know as they greet us. We finally get a table and I take off my jacket, still holding it. As Trey holds my chair out for me, I feel my phone vibrate. I take my phone out and read the text.

"MJ just texted me and said she's here," I tell Trey.

"Okay, you wanna go to the door and wait for her? I'll wait here so no one takes this table."

"Alright. I'll be back."

I put my purse and jacket down by him and walked back to the entrance. Through a big crowd, I spot her and Ty. Once she sees me, she smiles widely and starts walking fast towards me. I start walking a little faster toward her too and we both hug while laughing, almost falling over. We pull away and smile at each other, looking each other up and down.

I take a step back. "Girl you look scrumptious!"

"Thank you! You look like a whole meal, okay?"

She scrunches her eyes at me through her glasses.

"I know," I laugh, "Thank you."

"Hey Bray," Ty gives me a hug. "You look beautiful."

I thank him and hug him back.

"Where's Trey?" MJ asks.

"He's inside making sure no one steals our table."

"It's four to a table?" she asks.

"Yeah."

"Alright, let's go." MJ says.

After MJ and Ty give the lady their ticket, we make our way back to Trey.

"Hey MJ, you look gorgeous." Trey gives her a hug.

"Thank you."

"Sup, Trey." Ty gives him a bro hug.

"Hey man."

"Alright, let's get this party started, now that MJ is here!"

We all laugh as a song we know comes on. We walk to the dance floor, where everyone comes crowding around, to sing the song. After hours of dancing and eating a few of the snacks they had, MJ and I tell the boys that we're going to the bathroom to check our blood sugar for the second time.

"102." I read my meter before putting it back inside my purse. "That should be fine."

MJ put hers back too. "Mine's 148."

"Let's take some more pictures."

We take a few, and when we're about to walk out, a girl bumps me without saying excuse me.

"I know this girl ain't just bump you and then gone keep walking like she ain't do nothin'." MJ says, then, to herself, she adds, "MJ, calm down."

"Excuse you." I say, which makes the girl turn around.

She looks at me and rolls her eyes.

Getting annoyed, I ask, "You gotta problem?"

"Yeah, I do." the girl looks me up and down.

I cross my arms as she begins to speak.

"Stay away from Trey, 'cause my friend and I like him."

I look at her with a blank stare and she takes that as a cue to continue.

"He doesn't need someone like you. What he needs is someone who matches his standards and-

"As far as I'm concerned, I meet his standards way more than you do. Otherwise he wouldn't have been here with me and I couldn't care at all about you and your 'friend' liking him because he's MY boyfriend and not yours...have good night." I give her a fake smile and wave.

I watch as she looks dumbfounded while folding her arms.

MJ follows behind me and says to her, "You lucky, chick...you're so lucky."

I look around. "I'on know who these girls think they are."

"I'm so tired of these nappy headed little-

"There goes Tyler." I try to avoid her seeing me. "...let's go."

I grab MJ's arm and lead her back to our table.

As we are about to reach our table, I feel someone tap my shoulder. Turning my head around, I roll my eyes seeing that it's Tyler.

Dang, she saw me.

"Ya know I think I saw someone else with that dress on, she wears it better."

I cannot believe she just said that...you know what, this is my night, don't let her get to you.

"It's a pity that you try to be like everyone else." she flips her hair. I watch as her friend beside her starts giggling and Tyler smirks.

I shake my head, getting more annoyed.

MJ puts her hand up. "I'm sorry, but why is the grinch that stole Christmas talking to us?"

I can't help but laugh realizing that Tyler has on a green dress that is way too short with a split down the middle on the chest area with green makeup on, resembling the grinch.

Tyler asks bluntly, "And who was talking to you?"

MJ is about to push her but I block her, reassuring her that I can handle her.

"Tyler, you're the only one here trying to be like everyone else. You're dressed like a thot, which I'm pretty sure if you sat down, would show your panties and for what? So a boy can notice you. Ever since I met you, you've been so insecure about yourself. Being jealous of me because people were complimenting me on my clothes and not you, being mad at the fact that the same boy you liked, liked me instead of you, and in the entire friendship we had...not even realizing it, I let you push me around. The only thing I could think is that I finally found a friend, someone I could actually confide in, but you were so jealous of me and only cared about yourself, that you broke our friendship. Now that we've grown a bit, I thought that you would've changed but you're still the same. It's your loss because I'm one of the best friends you'd ever have." I hunch my shoulders. "Thanks to you, I now have my best friend and I now know what it feels like to put your fifty in the friendship and that person put theirs. Don't start stuff if you can't finish it, Tyler. The next time you wanna talk mess, make sure you come back with Jesus in your heart. Then, you'd actually be competing. Goodbye."

I turn around, heading back to our table and left Tyler dumbfounded. MJ flips Tyler off and I tell her to come on while laughing a bit. MJ puts her arm over my shoulder and pushes me a little, telling me she's proud of me.

"Girl!" she shouts. "Did you see the look on her face?" MJ laughs.

I laugh too.

"Hey, you okay?" Trey asks.

I say in delight, "Actually, I'm better than okay."

"Bray just clowned the mess out of Tyler." MJ laughs.

Trey looks down at me. "That's my girl." he wraps his arm around me.

I can't help but smile.

After a while, Trey and I lose Ty and MJ and we're all alone.

"Have I told you how beautiful you are?"

"Yes. Like 40 times already." I say, exaggerate.

He smiles then laughs.

I put my arms around him. "I don't mind it though."

"Oh really?" he says sarcastically while biting his lips and putting his arms around my waist.

I smile as his eyes flicker down to my lips. I quickly look away from him and rest my head on his chest. I hear a small chuckle from him.

"Dance with me?" he asks.

"Of course."

We go to the dance floor and slow dance. Halfway through the song, I feel a weird sensation go through my body.

"Woah...You okay?" he asks worriedly as I lose my balance.

I feel myself get dizzy. "Yeah, I just feel tired all of a sudden. I don't know what's happening."

"Yeah, you look really tired. Come on, let's sit down."

"O-

And everything goes black.

Chapter Eleven The Hospital

"He will cover you with his feathers, and under his wings you will find refuge; his faithfulness will be your shield and rampart."
Psalm 91:4.

I hear a slow beeping sound getting louder and louder as I start to wake.

Where am I?

Making sure I didn't break anything, I slowly wiggle my toes, fingers, and move my eyes around. I then feel something in the elbow of my arm.

Why am I in a hospital? Whatever happened…I thank you Jesus that I'm okay, I pray.

Finally knowing where I am, I slowly open my eyes, finding it hard to keep them open. When I'm able to open them fully, I look around to see myself under the covers in a hospital bed. I slowly turn my head to see an I.V. in my arm. I look to the left of me to see what looks to be my homecoming dress.

Homecoming…the only thing I remember is being at homecoming, so what the heck happened?

I continue looking around realizing bouquets of flowers and teddy bears are everywhere. I slowly turn my head when I hear a toilet flush from across the room. Waiting for the person to come out, I try my hardest to keep my eyes open. My mom comes out and grabs her phone, not noticing I'm awake.

"Mom."

"Bray!" she scurries to me. "Hi baby."

I crack a smile. "Hey mommy."

"How are you feeling?" she asks.

I yawn. "Tired."

"You can barely keep your eyes open." she says, worriedly.

"Mom…what happened? Why am I here? The only thing I remember is being at homecoming…"

"Your blood sugar dropped low while you were at homecoming."

What? For real?

I frown a little, getting mad at myself as she continues.

"You passed out and went into a coma."

"What was my sugar?"

"22 and it kept dropping."

"That's the lowest it's ever been." I rub my head and take a deep breath. "…I'm glad I woke up."

"Me too." she gives me a big hug.

I hug her back and start to cry a little.

"I'm so glad you're okay Bray." she continues to hug me and I can't help but feel guilty.

How did I not make sure my sugar was okay? I can't believe this actually happened. I should've been more responsible!

All these thoughts consumed me as I continued to hug my mom.

"I'm so sorry, mom."

She pulls away. "For what?"

"I should've been more responsible. My sugar was fine and I-I don't know what happened…"

"Bray, it's okay. We'll talk about it another time and don't worry, we praise the Lord that you woke up."

"Yeah."

I look at her and smile as a tear slides down her cheek. She gives me a sad smile and I pull her back into a tight hug. For five minutes we sit and hug each other without saying anything and I say a long prayer in my head. Breaking the silence I ask where my sisters are.

"Brii just drove them back home a little bit before you woke up," she pulls away.

"Okay..."

She smiles. "You have someone waiting to see you."

"Trey?" I ask.

She nods. "He's been here since last night and hasn't left."

I half smile and she gets up and goes over to her phone.

"Earlier, he had gone home to wash up and stuff."

"What about MJ?" I ask and I notice her face suddenly drops.

"Um..."

"What's wrong?"

"She's here in the hospital but..."

What? Why?

"Mom...you're starting to scare me."

"After homecoming, she went back home and had a breakdown..."

What?

"Her blood sugar went up a bit too high, so she's here."

"Is she awake?"

She shakes her head. "Mary left to her room not too long ago."

I look up at the ceiling. My breathing begins to increase.

Please God, let her wake up.

"Don't worry Bray, she will be okay."

"It's just this hasn't happened to her in a few weeks. Ever since the party, she'd been doing better. I can't help but feel guilty."

"Don't. You know MJ, she's a fighter. She will wake up."

I nod.

"If you're not feeling up to it, Trey can see you tomorrow."

"No, it's okay, I'll see him now. How long have I been here?"

"Just a day." she says.

"What time is it?"

She walks over to her phone. "7:46 p.m. You know Bray, I really like Trey. He really cares about you and he told me a few things about himself and his family. He's a good kid."

I smile shyly as she comes back to my bedside. "Yeah…"

She pulls me into a hug and I hug her back tightly.

"Thank God you're okay." she says. "I told everyone, and they sent prayers for you. Everyone was so worried. Poppa and a few others came to visit, that's who all this is from."

I look around and smile at the pretty flowers.

"A few are from your friends from the club too."

"Thanks mom. I love you."

"I love you too. Do you feel up to washing up and stuff?"

"Yeah, I'll do that before you tell him I'm up."

"Okay."

20 minutes later…

Trey runs to me. "Bray!"

"Heyy." he hugs me and I smile feeling comfort.

"I gotta call Brii, so I'll be in the hallway." my mom says.

"Okay." I say.

She walks out the room and leaves the door halfway open.

He pulls away and slides his hands to mine, giving them a kiss.

"How are you feeling?"

"I'm okay, just tired still."

"Yeah…I'm glad you're awake."

"Me too." I pull him into another hug and he wraps his arms around me tightly, making sure to not touch the IV.

"I was really worried," he says.

"My mom told me you stayed the whole night."

"Yeah, I didn't wanna leave until I knew you were okay…" He slowly loosens his grip and I pull away to look at him. "But my mom and yours insisted I go home and change." he rolls eyes in a playful way. "My family and I prayed for you. We were all so worried."

I look down.

"I- I was scared that if you didn't wake up…" he starts to get teary eyed and looks down. "I prayed and prayed…"

"Hey…" I cup his face. "I'm alive and okay."

He continues to look down.

"Trey, look at me…"

He slowly lifts his head. Seeing his usually bright, brown, and green eyes look dull, with guilt, pain, and tears, breaks me.

"I'm okay."

He gives me a sad smile and I wipe a tear from his cheek.

"Don't cry," I wipe away another tear.

He grabs a hold of my hands and brings it in front of him.

"Why do you have so many band aids on your fingers?" he rubs the back of my hands.

"Nurses had to prick my fingers while I was asleep, to make sure my blood sugar wouldn't drop again. Their prickers hurt way more." I say.

He looks back up at me.

I laugh, "You know what they say, when life gives you lemons, you make lemonade…with Splenda."

He narrows his eyes and furrows his eyebrows in confusion.

"You get it? 'Cause Splenda is sugar free." I crack a laugh to try to lighten the mood. He begins to laugh while shaking his head.

"You're so random sometimes." he caresses my hair. "You would try to joke with the situation we're in."

He cups my face with his right hand and I lean my head into it.

"You, almost dy-" his voice cracks. "Me, almost losing you."

I look him in his eyes. "Thanks for being here." I feel myself getting teary eyed.

He pulls me into a hug again. "You don't have to thank me. I'll always be here."

How did I get so lucky?

Trey says something, snapping me out of my thoughts.

"Huh?" I quickly say, pulling away from the hug.

"I said, 'Everyone from the club hopes you're okay.' Mary-Kate is down the hall, actually."

"She is?"

"Yeah."

"Why? What happened to her?"

What the heck? What is going on?

"She said she had pain in her neck."

"Oh wow, I hope she's okay."

"She looked fine."

"Okay."

After a few seconds, he says, "I think visiting time is almost over."

"Yeah, I know you have to get back home. I think my sisters can't come back tonight either."

He smiles. "Your sisters are so funny. They were telling me stories about you and them."

"Oh lord," I put my hand on my face, which made him laugh.

He teases. "I didn't know you guys had a YouTube channel."

"Yeah. We just haven't posted a new video yet because school started," I shrug.

"I watched 'em. You guys are pretty entertaining."

"Thank you. Can you pass me my phone please?"

Trey gets up and grabs my phone from the desk. He smiles while looking at my lock screen.

"I forgot, who took that picture of us again at the carnival?"

I roll my eyes. "Balice did, right before you chased me around for taking one of your Slim Jim's." he laughs.

"I don't play when it comes to my Slim Jim's."

"And I don't play when it comes to my ice cream."

He hands me my phone. "She did good with the pic though."

"Yeah, she did…Oh my Gosh, I have 29 text messages and 104 on Snapchat."

He gives me a soft smile and I start to feel a type of way.

"I'm sorry." I say, feeling guilty.

He frowns. "For what?"

"I know this isn't how you wanted our first month anniversary to go. Me being in the hospital and you worrying."

"Bray," he says sternly.

I look at him as he looks at me seriously.

"Shut up…I don't-"

He catches himself and turns his head to the door where my mom is talking on the phone. "I don't care about any of that." he sighs and brings his attention back to me.

He comes and sits beside me on the bed and cups my face. "The only thing I care about is your health. I will be here day and night to make sure you're okay."

I frown. "But this is the one thing I didn't want to happen. I knew eventually something would happen, -not this bad though- but I knew I would be a burden to you sooner or later." I start to ramble. "Look at you, you're here in a hospital worrying if your girlfriend is alive or not. That's so much to put on someone. I was surprised you still wanted to be with me after you found out I was diabetic."

He looks taken aback before speaking. "Bray, you would never be a burden to me, ever."

Tears fall from my eyes.

"Being a diabetic makes you no different."

"But it does!" I exclaim. "Being a diabetic is like having to live everyday like it's your last. You never know when that high or low blood sugar will be your last. If you have too much sugar in you or too little, you feel all these crazy things. My doctors still tell me that I'm in the honeymoon period even though I've had it for a while now. So I sometimes can't catch how I feel and that's when the people who truly care about me step in. Look what happened. Other people wouldn't care to check on me.

"Well, I'm not like other people, Bray. It never mattered to me that you have diabetes, and it never will." he looks me in my eyes. "I got you."

I grin. "And I got you."

"Bray, I...I l-

My mom walks into the room. "Bray, your sisters are on the phone."

She hands me the phone and Trey and I talk to them for at least 30 minutes. Afterwards, visiting time is over, and Trey leaves.

"Mom? Hey Mom, is it okay if I go down the hall and check on Mary-Kate?"

"She could be asleep."

"She's not." I hold up the phone. "She just posted something on Snapchat."

"Are you sure you're feeling up to it?"

"Yes. I'm okay."

She comes over and helps me stand. I grab a flower from a vase to give to Mary-Kate. Dragging the I.V machine with me, I slowly walk five rooms down the hallway to Mary-Kate's room. I knock on the door and a beautiful woman with blonde and brown highlights, and bright blue eyes opens the door.

"Hi. Can I help you?" the woman says.

"Hi. I don't know if you remember me from the carnival, but my name is Bray and I'm a friend of Mary-Kate's. I just wanted to check up on her and see how she's doing."

"Oh, yeah, of course. How could I forget? Come on in. Mary-Kate, you have someone here to see you."

I give her a half smile. "Heyy."

"Hey, Bray. What are you doing here in the hospital?"

"Well, I sorta had a mishap at homecoming."

She looks at me confused.

"What about you? I just found out today you were in here."

"Yeah…"

I stop in my tracks as I see a huge lump on the side of her neck. My mouth falls into an 'o' and I quickly recover and look at the bed.

Her eyes drop. "Um, I-"

I whisper. "We don't have to talk about it."

"Okay," she breathes.

There's a knock on the door. Mary-Kate's sister goes and opens it.

"Hi, I just wanted to introduce myself. My name is Bahati Fletcher. I'm Bray's mom."

"Hi, it's nice to meet you. I'm Mary-Kate's older sister, Miranda."

"Oh hi, I think I remember seeing you at the carnival."

"Yeah. That was me." she says. "Mary-Kate talks about Bray all the time. She's a really brave young girl."

"Oh, thank you." Mom smiles and shares a look with me and MK. "Bray has told me a few things about Mary-Kate, too. She's an angel."

"Thank you," Mary-Kate says.

"Wanna go out in the hallway?" Miranda asks.

Mom smiles. "Yeah."

She shuts the door.

I smile. "You two look just alike."

She giggles. "Oh, yeah."

"Where's your mom and dad?"

"Well my dad's at home with my little brothers and my mom…she passed away."

"Oh, wow. I'm so sorry."

"It's okay. I know I'll see her one day."

I gesture toward the edge of the bed and Mary-Kate nods.

"How did she die?"

"Cancer. Thyroid cancer to be exact."

I look at her sincerely and she gives me a sad smile.

I whisper. "I'm so sorry."

"It's okay, Bray. Now tell me what happened at homecoming," she demands.

"Well, from what my mom and Trey told me," I shrug, "I passed out at homecoming and went into a coma from my blood sugar being extremely low."

"Wow, Bray, I'm so sorry."

I smile. "It's okay. I woke up a day later with no memory of passing out and I'm surrounded by all these beautiful bouquets of flowers and stuffed animals."

"Aw, Bray." she says.

I run my hands through my hair.

"We can talk about it."

I shake my head.

She's dealing with a lot herself right now.

She insists and I pause for a second.

"My mom was so worried. I'd never seen her look so scared and broken before…" My eyes tear up again. "My sisters were so happy to see me through FaceTime. I just wish I could've hugged them. But we joked and laughed and- I just wish they were here. Trey stayed the whole night so he could be here when I woke up." I smile to myself. "All my other family and friends are happy I'm awake."

"Bray. Are you okay? For real?" she gives me a worried and sincere look. I look at her, try to smile, but shake my head. I start crying and cover my face with my hands.

"I can't believe this actually happened. I-I could've died, Mary-Kate. I made my mom so worried and my sisters... I thought my sugar was okay and it dropped. I mean, I know it does that often for me, but... I should've been more responsible-"

"You can't blame yourself for this. It's not your fault. I mean, I know that people with diabetes have a honeymoon period, so you can't blame yourself."

"It's just actually realizing... I've been asleep for a day. There was a possibility of me not waking up." I wipe my tears.

"You can't think like that, Bray. Remember when I said my mom would tell me a scripture?"

I think to myself. "No," I sniff.

She giggles. "She would say, 'She laughs without fear of the future'. So you may not know what tomorrow will bring but you have to continue to be happy."

I give a sad smile.

"And hey, it was only through God that you woke up anyway. And if you didn't, it was just time for you to go home. But obviously you still got some things to do in this world."

I laugh a bit and say, "So do you."

Mary-Kate gives a sad smile. "Eh, I think my time is coming to an end."

"Don't say that...you're gonna live a long life."

She hunches her shoulders. "Yeah. But I think I did okay. I had a sweet sixteen…sort of. I met you and Kevin and everyone else from the club."

"Kevin?" I ask suspiciously with a smile on my face.

"Yeah…I like him but I know he likes you still."

"Well you have nothing to worry about. I'm happy with Trey."

"You should be. Trey's a really great guy and you deserve each other."

"Thanks." I smile, "I'm so glad I met you, Mary-Kate. All those times of us talking on the phone really helped me, and I- I wanna say thank you for being such a great friend."

"Thank you. And thank you for being someone I could talk to."

"No problem…well, I'm gonna let you get some rest and I'll see you later."

"Yeah, you get some rest too."

I smile and she pulls me into a tight hug. I smile, returning it.

"You're a great friend Bray…anyone would be lucky to have you."

I smile even more as tears fall from my eyes.

"Anyone would be lucky to have you too." I pull away, "Ah, I'm so emotional. This is for you." I hand her the flower after keeping it behind my back.

She smiles and I can see tears in her eyes.

"Thank you."

I head towards the door.

"See you soon Bray."

210

"Goodnight, Mary-Kate."

"Night."

I close the door and start walking with my mom to my room with the I.V. I stop walking, thinking of the conversation I had with Mary-Kate. A weird feeling comes over me.

"You okay?"

"Yes."

I look back at Mary-Kate's room. My attention is now drawn to three nurses running down the hallway to the elevators. I listen in on their conversation as one of them mentions MJ's name and worry takes over me.

"What? What's wrong with MJ?"

"I don't know, Bray." I look up at my mom as she watches the nurses.

A nurse starts talking through a walkie talkie and I try my best to listen.

"Yeah, we're on our way now. She's not breathing? We're coming now."

I immediately start walking to follow the nurses. My mom notices and holds onto me. I try my hardest to get out of her grip as my breathing increases by the second. I hear her call my name, but her voice starts to fade as fear takes over me.

Chapter Twelve The Funeral

"Jesus said to her, 'I am the resurrection and the life. The one who believes in me will live, even though they die; and whoever lives by believing in me will never die. Do you believe this?'"
John 11:25-26.

"Ready to go back to school?" my mom asks me.

"Wish I wasn't even going. I haven't been since the day before homecoming." I sigh while fixing my hair. "What's one more day?"

"Yeah, but-"

"And I have to get ready for later on anyway."

Mom gives me a sad smile. "It doesn't start 'till 5:30, Bray."

I slowly put my hands over my face and begin to cry. I feel her against me as she pulls me into a tight hug. I move my hands from my face and hug her back.

"You gotta go get all the work you missed. I'm going to pick you up early, though." she hugs me again.

"I can't believe she's gone."

She pulls away and looks at me. "I know, Bray, but you know where she's going, right?"

I nod.

"Don't shed another tear, baby."

She gives me a kiss on my forehead. I pull away and grab my earrings.

"I gotta help Bailey, Bray."

I nod. She walks out of my room and I wipe away my tears.

"Let's get this over with," I sigh.

During 7th period, I'm walking with Trey to my next class, I feel someone tap my shoulder. I turn around and let go of Trey's hand, to see Tyler looking at me.

"Look, Tyler, I am not in the mood today."

"I know, Bray," she says. "Can I talk to you for a second?"

I look at her, trying to figure out if she's serious. "Um, sure." I look back at Trey. I mouth 'it's okay' and he continues to eye Tyler suspiciously.

"I know you just got out of the hospital. How are you feeling?"

I stare at her. "I'm okay."

"I just...wanted to say I'm sorry for how I've been acting. I know I've been mean but I just wanted to make sure you were okay."

I give her a half-smile.

"And I guess I wanted to get this off my chest too. You're really lucky to have Trey. And MJ. No, scratch that, they're lucky to have you."

I look at her, shocked.

Did she really just say that?

"Wow, uh...thanks, Tyler."

She smiles. "You're welcome." and walks away.

I slowly turn around and walk towards Trey.

"What did she want?" he asks.

"To apologize," I say shocked with a little smile on my face.

"Really?"

"Yeah."

"Wow."

I close my eyes and take a big sigh.

"You okay?" Trey asks.

"Yeah. I'm fine."

He looks at me uncertainly.

I change the subject. "Let's get to class."

"Alright see you later baby girl," Trey gives me a kiss on the cheek. "We'll talk about it tomorrow." he whispers in my ear.

I slowly nod and walk into class.

At home after school…

I look at the mirror and apply some red lipstick on. I check myself out one more time before going back into my room. I sit on my bed and check my phone. I smile sadly seeing my home screen picture of the club. I take a deep breath and grab my purse, before going downstairs.

"BRAY, MAKE SURE TO PACK YOUR LANTUS JUST IN CASE!" my mom yells down.

"OKAY."

I go into the kitchen, finding Balice looking in the refrigerator.

"Girl you scared me. What are you doing?" I ask, leaning against the wall.

She side-eyes me. "Getting some water."

She closes the fridge and walks out. I go over to the refrigerator and open the freezer. I grab my freezer bag and get my insulin from the fridge. I place it inside the bag, along with my pin needles, carb book, alcohol swabs, water, and a few snacks. I walk back into the living room seeing everyone downstairs already.

Mom asks, "You ready, Bray?"

"Yeah…oh shoot, I forgot my sweater upstairs."

I run upstairs to my room and grab my sweater. I come back down and we all walk out of the house to the car. We drive for an hour and a half before arriving at the funeral home. I get out of the car, feeling my whole mood get even worse than before. I go to the trunk along with Balice and my mom to help get Bailey's wheelchair out. Brii lifts her out of the car and places her in the wheelchair. Going inside, I smile shyly as the ushers greet us. Going into the room, there is a man playing a piano. Not a lot of people are there.

Mom says to my sisters. "You guys can go sit there."

I keep my eyes locked on the casket as my mom and I walk down the aisle. I feel myself start to cry as we approach it more and more.

She looks so peaceful.

I feel more and more tears running down my face.

"I'm gonna miss you Mary-Kate. Thanks for being a great friend… see you again in heaven."

I turn around and as I'm about to walk away, I spot my friends on the benches looking at me. I walk over to them, and Corey pulls me into a big hug. I then felt smothered, and I realized that we're all standing in a group hug. I feel myself cry harder than I did before. I sit down next to MJ and she lays her head on my shoulder as I place mine on hers. Two hours have gone by after the pastor,

Mary-Kate's dad, her sister and other family members walked up to the podium. Now it's my time to go up.

I clear my throat. "Hello everyone."

They say hello back.

"I'm a little nervous right now. Mary-Kate's dad and sister asked me to speak a few days ago and I was really shocked and honored." I smile shyly.

I look at her dad, little brother, and sister to see them half smiling.

"But, um…Mary-Kate was a really awesome, beautiful person. I had only known her for a few weeks, and she was always a positive person. At first when I met her, she was kind of shy but getting to know her, we had a lot in common. And not just me but with Rachelle, Corey, MJ, Ty, Kayla, and especially Kevin and Chanel." I smile a bit at the end. "I don't know if most of you know, but Mary-Kate was in the National Illness club at Lakeside Hospital. The people I named are in it too…I am myself. Even though she had just become a part of it, she was already family. She told me that being in the club was one of the best things that had ever happened to her. That everyone in it was a blessing." I look down for a second. "She told me that I was a beautiful, brave person, and that I need to keep being myself because the Lord's light shines through me…" Tears stroll down my cheeks. "I- I was so humbled and I didn't understand why she would tell me things like that...it made me think back to one night when I was praying. I prayed that something really great would come into my life and make things better…That was Mary-Kate. She was the angel I asked for." I started pouring down crying, covering my face. I wipe my tears and look around the room. To Mr. Daniels, I say, "Your daughter was an angel and she will be missed."

Walking back down, I stop to give Mr. Daniels and Miranda a hug. Mary-Kate's brother smiles at me and I return one. Going to my seat with my family, people gave me a rub on my back. Just then, a beautiful lady with dark brown skin and curly brown hair made her way to the microphone on the stage. She begins to sing *Pretty Bird* by Crooked Still, as a piano and violinist begin to play. I smile listening to the lady sing. After the service, everyone gets into their cars to make their way to the cemetery and some to the repass. My family and I drove straight to the repass.

"That should be only for the family," my mom says, "And Bray, your speech was really good."

I half smile. "Thanks, mom."

She gives me a side hug as we walk into the banquet. I push Bailey's wheelchair into a space in the table.

"Thanks Bray," she says.

"You're welcome," I say.

Brii says. "I'm just saying though…this is a really nice haul."

Balice takes off her coat. "Right. I was thinking the same."

"Yeah, turns out her family is really wealthy," I say in a whisper-like tone while scratching my head.

"Really?" my mom questions.

"Yeah."

"Hmm." they say.

Balice smiles. "That's cool."

I nod and look around to see Nurse Belsh walking in. I walk over, meeting her at the table next to us.

I smile a bit. "Hey, Nurse Belsh,"

"Hey Bray. You look very pretty."

"Thank you," I say, "So do you."

"Thank you. How are you doing?" she asks.

I look down as I feel myself starting to tear up. "I'll be okay."

She nods. "Come here."

She pulls me into a tight hug. I sigh as she rubs my back.

"It's gonna be okay," she says. "You know where she's going."

I look up at her and she smiles down at me.

"I'm gonna miss her."

"We all are. She'll forever be a part of the club."

I giggle a bit. "Yeah."

"Remember when we had the little trivia game a few Saturdays ago and she won every time?"

I laugh. "Yes, she knew all the answers to every ONE."

Nurse Belsh shrugs with a smile on her face. "She really was a Miss know-it-all."

"She was."

"Bray."

I look behind me to see Kayla and Ty walking towards me.

I give them both a hug. "Hey guys,"

"Hey," they both say.

I pull away to see them smiling sadly at me with tears in their eyes.

"You okay?" asks Kayla.

"I will be. You?" I look at the both of them.

"We will be." they look at each other, then back at me.

I grab their hands and squeeze and we laugh while hugging each other again. I look behind them to see MJ, Chanel, Rachelle, Kevin, and Corey walking in with a lot more people following after.

We all stood in a circle and smiled at each other. I start crying as we all hug one another. I hug Rachelle first.

She will always be a person I can trust.

Crying even more we pull away.

"I'm so glad that you're okay, Bray."

"Oh, yeah, I'm fine."

She smiles sincerely. "Thanks, Bray,"

"For what?" I ask, confused.

"For being an awesome friend."

"You're an awesome friend." We smile at each other.

She walks away and I feel someone put their arm around me.

"My chicken nugget," Corey laughs.

I gasp playfully.

"I'm not even the shortest one out of us, it's MJ."

"You're so dramatic, Bray," he says.

"You love it though."

I laugh as he gives me a big hug.

I think I'll always look up to him as a big brother.

He picks me up off the ground as he gives me a tight squeeze.

"Are you trying to break me?" I say while my mouth is muffled by his shoulder.

"Yeah," he simply says. "For going into a coma."

He sits me down and I pull away to see that he's serious.

"Don't do that again, Bray." his eyes fall to the ground and back to mine.

"It wasn't intentional." I mumble, feeling guilty.

"I know. You scared me. I'm just so happy that you're okay."

I smile and he gives me another hug.

We both giggle, pulling away, and Chanel and Kayla walk up to me. The three of us quickly pull each other into a hug.

I'll always love these two. Chanel, the conceited but caring one and Kayla the mean and hyper one.

We pull away, wiping our tears.

"If you ever go into a coma again. I will smack you." Kayla says with a straight face. "Literally will smack the fudge out of you."

"I think she gets it Kay." Chanel says, "But seriously, we're glad you're okay. We just lost one friend, we don't need to lose another."

I smile. "I love you guys."

"I love you too," they both say.

They both put a hand on my shoulder before walking away. I suddenly feel someone hit my forehead from behind.

"Really Ty?" I ask annoyed but happy at the same time.

"That's for going into a coma."

I try to hit him back but he keeps moving my hands down to block me.

"You'll never be tall enough to reach me, Bray."

"Um, I can jump pretty high, so…"

"In your dreams," he says.

I laugh and he pulls me into a hug.

Someone I can joke around with.

We pull away and he gives me a big smile.

"How are you doing?" he asks.

"I'm okay. Just today and the last few days have been hard."

"Yeah, I understand." he smiles sadly. "I'm boutta go get me some food so…I'll catch you around."

I laugh and tell him to try not to eat everything. He laughs and says, "no promises."

I turn around and MJ pulls me into a tight hug, taking me by surprise. I hug her back and start to cry again. I feel her tears drop on my shirt as she squeezes me tighter.

Man I love this girl, my best friend.

Staying there for what seemed like forever, we finally pull away. I smile lightly as she takes off her glasses and wipes her tears.

"Sorry." she says, "for getting your shirt wet."

"It's okay. I did the same to yours." I laugh it off

She looks up at me with tears strolling down her cheeks. "You know, this taught me something…"

I give her a concerned look.

"To never take things for granted. We never know when anything could happen to us. God could take any of us while we're in the middle of eating noodles, and you know what? That would be okay but we would wish for more time. Bray…" she starts to cry even more.

"At one point of time, I thought that I wasn't good enough to be on this Earth and then I realized…I may not have everything in this world but at least I'm breathing right now. You know. I have my mom, your mom, my brother, this club, and my best friend."

I knew I shouldn't have put on mascara. I wipe carefully under my eyes.

"As far as I'm concerned…I'm already healed. I'm tired of letting diabetes control my way of thinking. Diabetes is a name and Jesus is above every name and as long as I have Him…I'm not going to worry."

I pull her into a tight hug and we start crying tears of joy, guilt, and sadness all at once.

"I'm lucky to have you as a friend too, MJ. You'll always be my best friend."

I pull away and we both smile. We do our handshake.

"Okay enough of the crying. It's making me hungry." she takes her glasses off and wipes her eyes.

I can't help but laugh.

"I'm serious though. I'm bout to get me a plate."

I giggle. "You and Ty are just alike."

"I know. That's why we're cute together."

Before MJ could take another step, Ty was in front of her with a plate for him and her.

She gasps and asks, "For me?"

"Of course baby."

"Aw, see, this is why I like you." MJ starts walking. "Catch you later Bray."

I smile and shake my head. I turn around to see Kevin finish talking to Chanel and gives her a hug. She walks away and he spots me looking at him. He smiles and walks over.

"Hey,"

He has his arms open.

"Hey," I open my arms and hug him.

We both pull away and smile.

"Your speech was beautiful. I already know Mary-Kate loved it."

I smile. "Thanks."

"You're welcome."

I say out of nowhere, "I don't want things to be awkward between us, Kevin."

He laughs a bit. "It's not, Bray, and it never will be."

I smile in relief.

"You're still my best friend," he says.

"And you are mine."

He hugs me once more and tells me he's going to get him something to eat. I do the same and I go back to the table where my family was to see that they have food already too.

"Imma tell Trey you hugging other boys, Bray."

"Shut up, Brii," I laugh, which makes them giggle.

As I'm about to sit down, I hear someone call my name. I turn around to see Miranda gesturing for me to come over. I sit my plate down and squeeze past a few people.

I give her a hug. "Hey Miranda."

She smiles. "Your speech was amazing. I know Mary-Kate was looking down, smiling."

I smile shyly. "Yeah."

"Hey Bray." Mr. Daniels says.

"Hey Mr. D." I say grinning, feeling myself get nervous.

"Nice speech. I really appreciate you doing that for us."

"Oh, it's no problem."

"And, uh, I have something for you.

I followed him closer to the wall. Not noticing it before, he holds out a medium sized bag.

"For you," he says.

"What's this?" I ask, curious. I look to see what's inside the gift bag.

"Think of it as an investment."

I see what looks to be a check.

A check to my mom…?

I grab it and gasp, reading the 5-digit number. I look back up at him and he smiles down at me.

I assure him. "Mr. Daniels I can't take this!"

"No it's fine, really. MK was gonna give it to you Saturday…" he drifts off and takes a deep breath. "She said you mentioned something about helping your mom get a restaurant started.

I gasp and think back to when she tried my mom's food.

"I think it was the time she brought a plate home. That food was so good. I haven't had food like that in a long time."

I laugh. "Thank you! My mom is over there if you wanna tell her."

"Yes, I will, but first," he scans the room. "Which boy is Kevin?" he asks suspiciously.

"Um…there." I point.

He looked over to Kevin and cleared his throat.

"Excuse me for a second Bray."

He starts walking off and I tell him thank you. He looks back and mouths a 'welcome'. I start looking through the bag again and notice a picture. I pull it out to see that it's a picture of Mary-Kate and I at the carnival. I smile and put it back in the bag before walking towards the table where my family sits waiting.

"What's that, Bray?" my mom asks.

"I'll show you when we get home," I smile eagerly.

She looks at me suspiciously. "Okay."

I sit down and say my grace before eating.

A little while after, I notice the sun going down and I head to a back window, away from everyone. Without anyone noticing, I walk out the back door to see a beautiful aisleway with a water fountain. Once around it, I found myself in the middle of a beautiful flower garden. I smile, looking around.

This. Is. Amazing.

I glance at every flower and lightly touch and smell a few. I walk further into the garden and take my phone out of my pocket to take many pictures. I stop walking when I notice my favorite flower of all, roses. I hurry across the pathway, almost running to the roses. I smile widely as I see red, pink, yellow and others. I sniff and take pictures of the roses. I stop as I see my favorite kind, the white rose.

Sniffing the white rose, I notice a blue one at the end of the bush.

I've never seen a blue rose before.

I keep my eyes focused on it and take a few pictures. From the corner of my eye I see something and nearly jump out of my skin as a light-toned lady in a beautiful white dress with long and flowing gray hair, comes up from the side of me.

She scared the mess out of me.

"Admiring the flowers?" she asks.

I still catch my breath. "Y-Yes."

"Know what they mean?" she looks at me and I notice her eyes are a bright hazel.

I softly say. "Yes mam."

She smiles. "Go on then."

"Red roses are a symbol of love, romance and beauty. Pink roses represent admiration, gentleness, gracefulness, and happiness. Yellow roses let someone know the joy they bring." I smile softly.

"Last but not least, my favorite of all…the white rose represents innocence, purity, and charm. When you give someone a white rose, you're saying *I'm worthy of you…*"

She grins at me. "And what about that one?" she points at the blue rose.

"To be honest, I've never even known there was a blue rose."

"Yeah, it's the rarest. Scientists actually experimented and created the blue gene to have the roses sprout blue."

"Wow, that's actually cool…in a way." I giggle a little, "Do you know what it means?"

"Yes. It represents poems, art and song."

"Beautiful. I just wish it was God's creation. I mean, if he wanted blue roses, there would have been."

"I agree." she looks at me. "Well I better be on my way, it was nice talking to you, Bray."

"Nice meeting- wait, how do you know my name?" I ask curiously.

She smiles softly.

"Keep your faith, Bray. Things will get better eventually. God has a plan for your life, this is only the beginning. Oh, and the boy you have is special. He could be the one." she winks at me and my mouth opens in shock.

She walks back to the main aisle and looks at me once more before disappearing around a corner.

"Wait." I hurry along to the aisle to find her nowhere in sight.

She couldn't have walked that fast, she was…old.

I scan the garden and I can't find her anywhere.

"Where is she?"

"Bray?" I hear my mom's voice. I look to the door and make my way around the fountain to her.

"I was looking for you."

"Yeah, I'm sorry, I just was looking at the flowers." I look around again.

"Well, come on inside."

"Wait, Mom. While you were walking over to this door, did you see a white lady with long gray hair and a white dress come inside by any chance?"

227

"No, no one was by the door." she looks at me. "Why? What's wrong?"

"Nothing. It was a lady out here and she talked to me for a sec and then just disappeared." I say confused. "She was an older lady. There are gates all around here so I thought she went back inside."

"Hm. Maybe she did. Come on."

We walk back in slowly and I scan the room to find her nowhere.

I wonder if she could be what I think she is...an angel.

***

I shoot awake from my sleep.

Was it all a dream? Oh my gosh, that felt so real...Mary-Kate...

I pick up my phone and read the time.

It's 2:55 A.M.

My mom begins shuffling around on the hospital bed next to the couch. She slowly awakes.

"You okay?"

"Yeah...had a weird dream." After a few seconds, "Um, is Mary-Kate still down the hall?"

She nods.

"Is MJ okay?"

"Yeah. What happened, Bray?"

I pause for a second and wipe a tear before telling Mom my dream.

Chapter Thirteen MJ

"Jesus went about all the cities and villages, teaching in their synagogues, and preaching the gospel of the kingdom, and healing every sickness and every disease among the people."
Mathew 9:35.

Monday morning will be a morning I'll never forget. That morning I remember feeling joy I've never felt before. I was in a coma. My best friend goes into a coma from low blood sugar and I go into one from high blood sugar. She stays low while I stay high...I was doing so well not having to go to the hospital as much as I would before. I listened to Bray and stopped doing irrational things. But after watching my best friend fall unconscious in front of me...I wasn't thinking clearly and thought of the worst but I should've known God would wake her up. She's got so much more things to do on this earth. That's what He told me Tuesday night. I laid there in the hospital bed hearing everything around me and suddenly I felt myself wake up. I was still in my hospital room. My mom was there holding my hand but then she slowly dissolved away, and I heard the door open. I slowly turned my head to a man. A man with brown skin and white hair. His face...it was slightly blurred. I couldn't see His face clearly and I became afraid.

Like what? Who is this man in my room? I am not the one to be messing with.

Then He spoke, "Don't be afraid."

I glanced at his wrists which had a tear in each of them. Knowing who He was, I immediately started crying. I grabbed His hands and brought them to my face. I kissed them and He pulled me into an embrace.

Between my cries, I said, "Are you here to take me home? Because I am all for it! I will be with you in paradise! Being with God and the angels and a pretty tiger…being able to eat anything I want!"

He smiled. "There's no eating in heaven."

"Oh…well that's okay, I know I'll have a lot to do."

I had begun to cry, thinking of my life here on earth. I paused, "You're not here to take me home, are you?"

He shook His head. "I have heard your prayers, MJ…I never forgot you. You believe in me. You have more knowledge about me than your friend and yet, you don't speak of me as much…why?"

"I-I…I guess I've been just…patiently waiting for my healing…I guess I just thought that I can't speak about you if I've never experienced anything with you."

Tears rolled down my face and I couldn't even look at Him. He's right. I shouldn't be ashamed to share the gospel. I grew up in the church, mainly going with my Auntie and I ended up becoming a diabetic at an age where I couldn't comprehend what was going on with me. I learn about Jesus and believe so hard that I will be healed but I fall silent…The woman with the issue of blood in the Bible was sick for many years! Became an outcast! She had enough faith that if she touched Jesus's clothes, she'd be healed. The man at the pool was crippled for years waiting for someone to help him get to the pool so he could get his healing but no one helped! No one except when Jesus came and healed him right where he was at! So what happened to me? Truth is…I didn't lose my faith but I thought I wasn't going to get healed so why would I say anything?

"I'm sorry. I'm so sorry."

He reached out and lifted my face. "Do you want to be made whole?"

I stared at Him.

"Yes…"

"Then believe…Tell everyone I am the healer. Healer of all manner of disease and sickness. I love you, MJ."

"I love you too. Are you sure I can't go with you?"

"I'm sure."

"What about Bray? She would like it better in heaven than here."

"Well she has a lot left to do on this earth…and so do you…all the members of the club do."

He smiled and walked away.

He dissolved right in front of me and I felt myself waking up from a dream. It felt so real. Jesus visited me in a dream. I fluttered my eyes open and it's dark in my room. I wiggled my toes as a nurse came over and checked my blood sugar without noticing I'm awake. I heard her mumble something to herself and she left. Seconds later, she came back with another nurse or doctor. The only light in the room was from the T.V. They had noticed I was awake since they stopped talking so abruptly but by this time, I really needed to pee.

"I need to pee." I said and they stared at me.

Did they not hear me? A girl gotta pee.

My mom snored kind of loudly which made me jump a bit. I started to rise up and the doctors helped me to the bathroom. They took a urine sample and I cuddled with my mom when I returned to my bed.

I told my mom the dream I had as we both ate yogurt and she held me to her chest. At least an hour later, the doctors called for my mom and they stepped outside my door. Seconds later they came back in. The female doctor looked at me with concern and a little bit of shock. I waited for them to speak.

"MJ...we got your urine test results...and...there's no ketones, like at all."

I said, "That means...?"

"MJ, your pancreas is functioning again...you're no longer a diabetic."

After those words left her mouth, my breathing started to increase. I quickly grabbed my meter, strips, and pricker to check blood sugar. I pulled off a band-aid from my pointer finger and checked my sugar.

"103. I accidentally ate all the yogurt without taking insulin."

OH MY GOSH.

"There's no way your blood sugar would still be normal after eating 32 grams of yogurt...how is this possible-

"Jesus...He healed me. He visited my dream and we talked and now I wake up...and I'm not a diabetic...Oh my gosh." I laughed while tears rolled down my face.

Suddenly, a brush of air traveled through the room and I watched as the nurse closed her eyes for a quick second. The nurse leaped for joy. "Yes...He did do this!" She repeated it as she left the room. My mom slowly walked to me with tears in her eyes. She sat on the bed and looked me in my eyes.

"Jesus did this for you?" I nodded and she looked down. "...I know I haven't been the best mother and I steered my life away from God but from now on, I will make Him first and make you a priority, MJ. I'm so sorry."

"It's okay, mom. I forgive you."

She pulled me into a tight hug.

"Let me get up off this bed so I can run down this hospital hallway and give thanks to God."

We both laughed and began to rejoice unto the Lord. *Jesus truly is my healer and I'm going to tell the world...Ahhh...I can eat ANYTHING I want. WHEN I want!*

Chapter Fourteen New Beginnings
10/21

"For I know the plans I have for you," declares the
LORD, 'plans to prosper you and not to harm you, plans to
give you hope and a future.'"
Jeremiah 29:11.

After my crazy dream in the hospital, it took me a
long time to go back to sleep that night. The next day, I
went to Mary-Kate's room and told her the whole story
after hugging her for five minutes straight. She was
shocked. She even told me she really was going to give me
money for my mom's restaurant.
Just wow!
I didn't get the chance to see MJ in her hospital bed
once she woke up, but she was able to come over to my
house a few days ago and I told her about the dream. Turns
out, she really was feeling depressed and no longer wanted
to be in this world. I thank God she didn't do anything! I
felt like such a terrible friend for not noticing the signs, but
she assured me to not feel that way...she said she was
doing a lot better and that she had big news. She just hasn't
told me yet.
Now, another Saturday has come, and it feels good
to be with my club members.
Nurse Belsh grabs a chair and sits. "Circle up
guys."
We all scoot our chairs to form a circle.

"...I know it's been a hard week. I hope everyone is doing better." Nurse Belsh glances at all of us.

I look around at everyone.

"First off...Bray, we're glad you finally decided to wake up. I hope that you're doing better and I hope that won't happen again."

"It won't." I say with reassurance.

She smiles and sighs. "Mary-Kate, you're feeling better?"

"Yes. A lot better."

"MJ?"

She smiles a bright smile. "I'm way better than good!"

"Okay. Let's go around the circle, see how everyone's been doing with their illness lately. Corey, do you want to go first?

"Sure."

Nurse Belsh has each of us share. I end up telling the group about my dream. They were shocked and a few cried.

After a few seconds, Ty asks, "Do you think any of us will die soon?"

I look down for a moment.

"No. I don't think any of you will." Nurse Belsh looks at MJ. "MJ, ready to tell them?"

MJ stands up and closes her eyes for a second. We wait for her to speak.

"Um...so ya know how we've been reading the Bible stories on healing, and I said my favorite was the woman with the issue of blood because she did everything she could as far as believing the gospel, spending all her money on seeing doctors, and becoming an outcast to everyone. The second she heard Jesus was in town, she had enough faith and believed that if she could just touch his garment, she'd be healed…" she pauses. "She had hope and I slowly learned to also…and I think that's why God…healed me."

I look at her confused as she takes out her blood sugar pouch and checks her blood sugar.

"92." she says and begins to guzzle a 16-ounce sprite bottle.

"Um MJ-

"Just wait." Nurse Belsh says and MJ stops drinking with only a little bit left in the bottle.

We wait 15 minutes and she checks her blood sugar. She looks up at us with tears in her eyes as she shows us her sugar. I gasp seeing the number.

"Oh my gosh!" I say.

"135." she says, "Through Jesus Christ stripes…I'm healed!" she breaks down.

Everyone begins to shout and cheer and I sit there replaying in my mind what she just did. There's no diabetic alive that has drunk that much pop whose blood sugar hasn't gone high from it!

Oh. My. Gosh. Oh my- MJ is healed! She's healed!

Nurse Belsh says, "Doesn't matter if you have cancer, or diabetes, or any disability or illness…Jesus is the only one who can heal you! Do not let your illness define you. Go and make a difference in the world." she adds, "You all are just in the waiting room, right now. Set only your faith in Jesus and He will heal you. Bray, you woke up from your coma. Mary-Kate, your tumor has gone down from your neck, Kevin, you ended up not needing the surgery and Ty, you finally got a job." she laughs a bit at the end.

We all laugh, and Ty rolls his eyes and smiles.

Tears have formed in my eyes as I stand up slowly and walk towards MJ. I pull her into a tight hug.

Thank you, Jesus! Thank you, thank you!

She whispers, "I'm sorry I didn't tell you sooner."

"I don't care..."

We pull away and I wipe her tears.

"Someone very wise said this, 'the life that we live is not just for us but for someone else too.'" Nurse Belsh winks at me, "MJ you're gonna be able to help a lot of people. You all will."

2 hours later...

"Alright, guys. Are you ready for your first meeting?"

"Is it okay that I'm kind of nervous?" I ask.

"For what?" Nurse Belsh asks.

"Because we're about to talk to little kids. I hope they like me." I realize that makes me sound a little whiny.

"Bray, we're gonna do fine." MJ says, reassuring me.

"What if they won't like us?"

"Us?" MJ asks. "They'll love me."

I give her the 'really' look and she laughs as I roll my eyes.

"I'm just playing Bray...Everything's gonna be okay."

I believe her. "Okay."

I hate when my nerves get the best of me.

"You both are going to do great. Now get in there." Nurse Belsh demands us playfully.

"Can we pray real quick?" I ask.

"Of course."

Nurse Belsh says a quick prayer with us before we scurry to the front of the door. We try to step though at the same time and knock into each other.

We both say, "Ow."

"We both can't fit MJ." I say, sternly.

"Duh, I know that."

We both turn to walk through again but stop, not wanting to hurt ourselves again.

She rolls her eyes. "You go first."

I smile sarcastically before walking in. I scan the room to see three girls and two boys.

"Hi everyone. My name is MJ and this is Bray."

I smile and say, "Hello everyone."

"We are going to be over the Junior Illness Club."

"So um, to give more information about ourselves...I'm 14 years old and I am a type 1 diabetic." I turn to MJ.

"I'm also 14 and I used to be a type 1 diabetic like last week...I'm here as proof that you can all be healed through our father in heaven."

"Jesus?" A girl asks.

"Yes!"

The girl continues. "My mom tells me about him all the time. He visited my dream."

"I know Jesus too!" a boy stands up which makes me smile even more.

"Me too." another says.

"That's great you guys!" MJ says.

"Would anyone like to introduce themselves?" I ask, looking at everyone.

I watch as a few people looked at the ground and a few continued to look at us. After a few seconds more, a different boy from earlier stands up.

"H-Hi. My n-n-name is Brandon a-and I-I-Im 4."

"He's so adorable." MJ whispers.

I nod and keep smiling as he continues.

"I h-have diabetes too."

"You talk funny." a girl says, and Brandon starts to cry a bit.

"Hey! That was not a nice thing to say." I walk closer to the girl,

"What is your name?" I ask her.

"...Sierra," she says shyly.

"And what is your illness?"

"Cancer." she looks around at the others and I can see the hearing aids in her ears.

"...Sierra, you can't say mean things like that to people. You hurt his feelings."

"I didn't mean to. I'm sorry."

"Don't apologize to me, you need to apologize to him." I mentally scold myself for sounding like a butthole.

She needs to know it's not okay to pick on people, especially if they have an illness.

Sierra gives him a hug. "I'm sorry, Brandon,"

"It's okay." he smiles.

239

I grin as he hugs her back.

MJ whispers to me, "Dang Momma Bray." to the group she says, "When you come into this room, there will only be positive vibes and no negativity. You'll feel love." MJ sits on a chair.

Everyone smiles and more kids ask to introduce themselves. After the hour is over, MJ and I both stay to make sure each kid is picked up by their parents. While waiting for our moms to arrive, MJ and I sit in the waiting room by the doors.

I pull my phone out. "That went better than I expected."

"I told you Bray. We did great. I think we're gonna have this group for a long time."

"Me too. It was fun. I literally found my mini me."

"Right, Yanna is literally me at 5," MJ smirks.

I laugh. "Elena acted just like me."

"That boy Keith is so Ty, bro."

"Right. I was thinking that too."

We both laugh.

"I'm gonna enjoy doing this with you Bray...I'm just glad you wanted to do it with me too."

"Of course I would MJ. I know you want to be a nurse one day...You're my best friend, sis." I look at her and she tries to do a cute face but fails miserably.

She looks like Donatello...the 1990 turtle.

"Okay, don't EVER make that face again."

I laugh and playfully push her.

MJ points. "There goes my mom,"

"Alright girl, I'll see you Monday." I give her a hug and she hug me tightly. We do our handshake, and she walks to her mom's car. After a few seconds I pull out my phone to look at Instagram and I suddenly overhear a woman speaking.

"We're so late. We need to leave now. I can't believe you're not here. You promised you'd be here." the woman says.

I look up to see the walking talking on the phone.

"...whatever, I'll let you know what the doctor says."

"Mommy, I don't feel so good." a girl says from beside her.

Dang, I did not realize she was right there.

I continue to look on Instagram.

"What's wrong? Are you feeling those symptoms the doctor talked about? Do you feel shaky, sweaty?"

"Um...yes."

"Okay, let's check your blood sugar."

I glance up from my phone and stare at them. After checking the girl's blood sugar, the mom waits impatiently for the meter to beep after 5 seconds.

"Oh no, it's 69." I can hear the panic in her voice. "Okay, you have to eat 15 skittles."

I watch the lady open her bag and begin to dig around her purse.

"Oh no, I left the skittles at home. Oh my gosh."

Once I hear her say that, I open my purse and take out a zip block bag of skittles and I walk over to them.

"Excuse me, I have some skittles." I show her them.

She sighs in relief before saying, "Oh my gosh, thank you so much!"

I smile and hand the girl the skittles and she thanks me.

"I can't believe I left the house without her skittles. I'm a terrible mom."

"Hey don't beat yourself up. I used to forget my supplies all the time. One thing missing and forget about using any of it." I giggle.

"You're a diabetic?" she asks.

"Yes. 3 years."

"Wow. Brooklyn here has only been for 2 weeks."

"Wow…how's everything been going?" I turn to face her.

"Tough, very tough. We went to the hospital because she had a seizure only to find out it was due to low blood sugar. The doctor's kept us for two days and now her sugar keeps dropping. This is all so new and a lot to take in and I have to be responsible for her in another way now."

"Well, at least she can catch how she feels when her sugar drops. It helps for this exact reason."

She smiles slightly before whispering, "Can I ask you something?"

I whisper back. "Sure."

"Does it get easier? Do you ever get used to it?

"Well for some people…I don't think they'll ever get used to it. Diabetes is one of those things where you just have to put up with it. It's so irritating sometimes because I just want to eat without thinking about how much the food will affect me and other times…it either makes you question your life or makes you want to enjoy it even more…and I've been at both." I pause for a second. "But God is the reason I'm here today. Yeah, it's not perfect but it gets easier…my best friend was just healed from it this past week. She's had it since she was 5…Jesus healed her."

"Wow! That's amazing! Just this week?'

"This week." I smile.

"Wow…" she scratches the back of her head and sighs. "I know she ran up and down the halls screaming."

I laugh and she giggles with me. "Jesus is the only cure for any disease in the world."

She smiles.

"I believe you." To Brooklyn she says, "Okay, I think that was 15, Brook."

"Okay." she says and tries to hand me the skittles.

"No keep it, I have plenty at home. I'm boutta get something to eat anyway. Oh, by the way, the hospital just opened a Junior National Illness Club where children with different illnesses can come and learn how to cope with it. If Brooklyn would be interested. It's every Saturday at 3."

"Oh wow okay. We'll think about it. Thank you…the car is here, Brook. It was nice meeting you…"

"Bray."

"Bray. I'm Gina…God bless you."

"You too." Brooklyn gives me a hug and Gina smiles at me before walking out to their car. I smile to myself.

I live this life for other people…

I suddenly feel my phone vibrate and I look up to see my mom's car. I answer the phone and walk out to get into the car and my mom pulls off.

"How'd it go Bray?" she asks.

"Pretty good." I say, "everyone was pretty cool."

"That's good Bray, I'm so proud of you." she reaches out with one hand and rubs my shoulder.

"Thanks, Mom," I smile.

When I get home, I change my clothes and get started on homework. When I finish, I go into the twin's room. We start talking about YouTube video ideas. After we finish, I go back to my room and take out my art book. I grab my phone and scroll through my photo gallery for the blue rose from the garden. I find it and start sketching it. Then suddenly, the doorbell rings. My mom calls me down and I quickly put my stuff up and go downstairs to find my mom standing by the door with it open.

I look at mom. "Yes?"

She turns her head outside and I do the same. I smile once I see Trey leaning against his mom's SUV. I walk down the railing, and across my yard to Trey.

"Look at you," I smile. "Sauce is dripping." I laugh.

"Look at you lookin' fine in your army green sweatsuit." he licks his lips and smiles.

I giggle and stop in my tracks.

"Oh my gosh!" I gasp and smile. "You cut your hair."

He scratches his jaw. "Yeah."

I step closer and put my hand lightly on his hair. I bite my lip. "Got waves now, huh?"

"Yeah...Do you like it?"

"Yes, it looks good on you."

Almost too good, I giggle.

"You?" I drop my hand from his hair.

"Yeah. I wanted to try something different." he winks at me.

I smile. "Good."

"You look beautiful, Bray," he bites his lip.

"Thank you." I blush. "Wait, why are you here all dressed up?"

"Well…" he stops leaning on the car and takes a few steps to me, with his hands in his pockets.

"A month ago, from Sunday this week…I took you on our first date to JayR's-

"Oh my gosh! Our 1st month anniversary." I squeal. "I totally forgot! I'm so sorry."

"You were in the hospital Bray, there's nothing to be sorry about." he takes a step closer.

I smile, folding my arms.

"I was thinking we could celebrate it now."

I shrug. "I'd have to ask my mom. Saturdays and Friday nights are usually our movie nights."

"Your mom said it was fine." he nods his head towards her.

I turn and look back at my mom to see her standing in the doorway still. "You knew about this?" I yell out.

"Yeah." she hunches her shoulders. "We been planned it."

I shake my head with amusement and turn my head back to Trey. "Well, just let me get changed first-"

He smiles. "You don't even gotta change. You look perfect in that."

"Alright." I smile widely. "Let me grab my medicine and purse then."

"Alright."

I run back into the house and go upstairs to grab my phone, charger, blood sugar pouch, and I put all that inside my purse. I go into the bathroom to take off my mascara and put on some lip balm, then lip-gloss and I walk into the twin's room to let them know where I'm going. I head back downstairs and go to the kitchen to grab my insulin out of the refrigerator.

"You have all your supplies, right?" my mom asks. I answer her. "Yes."

"Strips? Needles? Lantus, just in case."

"Yeah I-" I pull out my blood sugar pouch and feel that something is missing. I open it to see the strips aren't in it.

"Must be on my bed."

I run upstairs to my room and find my strips on the nightstand. I grab them and go back downstairs.

I put the strips into my purse. "Hey, what time is Brii coming?"

"She should be back by the time you come back too. Okay. Are you giving Trey his present now or after y'all come back?"

"Imma wait till after."

"Okay." she says.

"How do I look?"

She walks closer to me and smiles.

"Like me."

I laugh and give her a hug.

"Soooo pretty Bray." she caresses her acrylic nails on me and I quickly pull away.

It feels so weird when she does that. In a ticklish way.

I fidget. "Don't do that."

"Have fun. Call me from time to time."

246

"Okay I will. I love you!" I yell back.

"Love you too."

Trey holds the door open for me and I get inside the car. Mr. Williams greets me, turns his car on, and pulls off. I watch as my mom waits at the door until we aren't in front of the house.

We drive to Cold Stone to get Ice Cream before going to Belle Isle. Mr. Williams lets Trey and I out the car, and before long we're walking around while eating our ice cream.

"Belle isle is so pretty." I take a nibble of vanilla ice cream with candy sprinkles.

"It is, isn't it? I used to come down here with my family all the time before my grandmother died. Haven't been back since."

"And you chose to come back for the first time in a while with me?"

He nods.

"Didn't wanna come with your family?" I ask, concerned.

"Naw…don't really feel like it's a family anymore." he clenches his jaw.

"I'm so sorry Trey. I wish there was something I could do."

"You are. You being here with me is all I could ask for."

I smile. "Same here."

We continue to walk slowly and I look over at the view of the sun setting.

"I'm shocked it's not that cold out here."

"Yeah. I think it's an Indian summer?"

"What's that?" I ask.

"It's when the weather of summer kind of prolongs into the fall, making September and October have warm weather." he glances up at me while eating his vanilla Ice Cream.

I say with amusement, "I wish that could happen every time."

He chuckles. "How have you been doing since homecoming?"

I sigh.

"Definitely wasn't planning on my first homecoming going the way it did, but I'm okay. My mom's been monitoring me a little bit more lately, well a lot more…and it's fine. I guess I really scared her…" I look at the scenery, "At first, everyone kept telling me it's okay and I know it is, but I couldn't believe that it actually happened. Like, I actually passed out from not having enough sugar in me. Stupid blood sugar keeps going down, and… I ONLY read things like that happening to people but all while I was in the hospital, I couldn't help but think of the worst." I feel tears starting to form.

"Bray." he puts his ice cream down on the ledge. He cups my face with both of his hands and I close my eyes.

"Hey, look at me."

I open my eyes as tears roll down my cheek.

"I'm okay. I talked it over with the club and I'm okay." I smile and look down. "Trey, MJ is healed. She really is healed…I'm so happy for her!" I smile in relief. "We always talked about how'd it'd be when we would get our healing and it happened. MJ getting healed…it's almost like I got healed too. Just to know that one day, I will no longer have to go through this…"

Trey smiles at me.

"You are such a brave girl, Bray. I believe your healing is coming too. Well, it's already here. *1st Peter 2:24* says 'by whose stripes, ye were healed'."

He looks into my eyes and wipes a tear away. I smile softly and grab his wrist as he continues to cup my face. He kisses my forehead and pulls me into a hug, holding me tightly. I smile, feeling comfort and safety as he holds me.

"I forgot to tell you, but my grandfather said that he was praying for you to get better."

"Aww, I'm gonna have to meet him." I giggle, "We're gonna have to set a date so my grandfather and yours can meet, too. But I call my granddad Poppa because he's like one of those really cool granddads. Like, he'll go bungee jumping and skydiving without thinking twice."

"Oh yeah, we gotta have them meet." he laughs and picks up his ice cream.

I start eating my ice cream again. "This sunset is beautiful."

He glances up at the sun and stops walking. He looks at me and something flashes through his eyes but I can't tell what.

"Follow me." he grabs my hand and runs, making me run also. We throw our empty cups of ice cream away and jog to the middle of a bridge.

I take deep breaths. "Where are we going?"

"Wait here."

I give him a confused and suspicious look as he quickly walks away. A few seconds later he walks back with his hands behind him. I look confused while trying to figure out what he's hiding. He is finally in front of me and brings his hands in front, holding a beautiful, fully bloomed, white rose.

"Okay this is definitely from a movie."

He laughs with me and takes a deep breath.

"Promise I'll stay here till the mornin'."

Oh. My. Gosh...he's singing. He's singing the song we danced to on our first date. 'My Only One' by Sebastian Yatra ft Isabela Merced.

He finishes singing with a smile.

I smile brightly, "You have an amazing voice."

"Thanks," he blushes.

"I wanted to give you this." he looks down at the rose before locking eyes with me.

"You're special, Bray. The last month has been the best because of you. I can't imagine my life without you now. I think about you all the time - if you've checked your blood sugar, if you took your insulin, if you're eating too much ice cream and bacon."

I giggle as he continues.

"And, just, wanting to know how you're feeling. I love your style, your hair, your smile." he grins. "And you got a pretty nice butt too."

I burst out laughing and he laughs with me.

"And how you're so positive and kind. Now, I don't know what the future may bring but I do know that I am in love with you and I know that we still have our whole lives ahead of us. But right now, I know that you are who I want to be with. You said that, to you, the flower means the thing that makes everything better. You are my flower, Bray."

I smile feeling tears form.

"Whenever you need me, I'll be here…I got you."

He hands me the rose. I smile and look down at it for a second. I sniff it and look back up at him. I wrap my arms around his neck. He then put his arms around my waist.

"And I got you." I smile. We press our foreheads together. "You make me so happy."

He moves his head from mine and looks me in my eyes. I slide my hands to his chest and raise my head to look at him.

"I know that we're young and all…" My words trail off for a second. "Is it okay to say that what we have…is love?"

He sighs and looks down for a second before bringing his eyes to mine. "As long as God is first…then, yeah."

"So much has happened this past week…"

He smiles softly as I continue.

"I don't know what will happen in the future but, considering the fact that I could've died, but didn't. I just want you to know…" I took in a breath, feeling myself getting more and more nervous. I look him in his eyes. "…I love you." I smile. Then, more confidently, I repeat it. "I love you."

His eyes light up and he smiles. I smile looking into his brown, with a touch of green eyes. He squeezes my waist a bit as he looks me in my eyes.

"You love me?" he asks with the biggest smile on his face.

"Yes."

"More than ice cream?" he asks.

"Just as much."

"More than the Dolan Twins?"

"Uh, imma have to think about that one." I laugh and his smile fades. "Actually, I don't think I got a chance to watch their new YouTube video this week. Yeppers, let me go watch it right now." I move my hands off of him and I turn around to walk away.

As I'm about to take a step, Trey quickly grabs my right hand and gently pulls me back to him. He presses his lips on mine. I'm surprised at first but I kiss him back. He wraps his arms around my waist as I slowly cup his face. We pull away and put our foreheads together.

My gosh.

"Trey-"

"Stop walking away." he breaths, in a low tone.

I smile and a thought crosses my mind of what Chanel said about boys. "You're gonna have a lot more worrying to do about me...you sure you want this?"

"That was a really dumb question, Bray. I may not be able to put my feet in your shoes and see what it's really like being a diabetic, but I'll always be here for you. Always." he looks me straight in my eyes.

I smile and he gives me a kiss on my cheek. We interlace fingers and start walking.

"Oh I forgot to ask you," he says. "How did your first club meeting go with the little kids?"

"It was great."

He grins. "Yeah?"

"Yeah." I smile to myself.

"That's great. And please don't say that about the Dolan Twins again." he pouts his lips.

"You're just mad 'cause they're better looking than you." I eye him as I pick my pace up.

"Oh bet?" he raises his eyebrows and stops walking.

"Bet."

He starts to jog. "You're gonna regret that."

"Bet I won't." I turn around and start running.

"Oh no you don't!" he yells from behind.

We run for at least a minute before he catches me and spins me around.

***

"Y'all ready to watch the movie?" I hear Balice yell from downstairs.

"Yeah. Just gimme one second." I wave through my phone. "I'll call you tomorrow, MJ."

"Alright sis, love you."

"Love you too." I hang up the phone.

I turn my head to see Mom standing by my door.

"Hey Mom."

"Hey Bray. Poppa wants to talk to you." she hands me the phone.

"...hey Poppa...Yes, I'm okay...I know, I'm sorry...you said you're gonna take us to dinner and see a movie?! Yay, that would be great. I'm looking forward to it...okay, I will...I love you too, bye." I give mom back her phone.

"You doing okay?"

"Yeah, Poppa just made me feel sad. He was worried."

She nods.

"I just wish I knew what was going on with MJ, mom. I feel like I should've been a better friend." I run my fingers through my hair. "It's just, I went through the same thing when I first got diabetes, but she helped me...and now...I'm so happy we have Jesus with us."

"Me too." she says. "Y'know...I'm so proud of you." she walks to the side of my bed. "You're very brave, Bray. To see you go through what you go through every day and you still have a smile on your face."

I smile softly.

"Nothing but the Holy Spirit in you. Come here." she opens her arms and I stand up and pull her into a big hug.

"I love you, Mom," I say.

"Love you too." she playfully starts tickling me and I jump back with a slight smile on my face.

"No."

She laughs. "Come on, let's go watch a movie."

"Okay. Gimme one sec."

"Alright." she leaves my room and goes downstairs.

I get off my bed and open the door to my patio and walk outside, feeling the chill air as it lightly touches my skin. I grab my rose from the vase and I look at it. I then look up at the sky to see a full moon and one star next to it. I say a prayer. I pray for my family. Nurse Belsh, Mary-Kate, Kevin, Rachelle, Ty, Corey, Chanel, Kayla, and MJ. I pray that Trey and his family will have peace in their home. I pray that things will get better for them. I thank Him for setting Mary-Kate in my life. I declare I am healed from this diabetes. That all diabetics out there fighting this disease are healed. I look at the flower in my hand and realized that God is the one who can make everything alright. He's the only one that loves me the most, cares for me the most, comforts me the most, and even chastises me when I do something wrong 'cause that's what fathers do. Through Jesus…I realized…He is my healer, my rose. My *Sanative Rose.* He's always been and always will be the one to make everything better. I smile and put my rose back in the vase. I look around before going back inside and closing the door. I grab my blood sugar pouch and my phone and head downstairs.

"What took you so long?" Brii asks, irritated a bit.

I shrug. "My bad, Brii."

I sit down on the couch and check my blood sugar.

"What is it Bray?" Mom asks.

I pull the strip out of the meter. "133."

"Your funnel cakes are on the table in the kitchen and there's ice cream." she says.

"Okay." I eagerly get up and make my way towards the kitchen to get my plate. I put a little extra powdered sugar on it before heading back to the living room.

"What movie we watching first?" Bailey asks.

"*God's Not Dead.*" Mom says.

"Ooh yay okay." Balice says.

I grab the remote as Balice gets up and slips the movie into the DVD player. I press play and the movie turns on. I smile, looking at my family as they eat their funnel cakes and bring their attention to the screen. Then, I feel a vibration from my phone. I pick it up to look at it, seeing it's a message from Trey.

It reads, "Goodnight beautiful. I know you're watching your movies."

I reply and say goodnight. I put my phone down and put my focus back on the movie.

"I love you guys," I say.

"Love you too," Balice says

"Love ya too," Brii says.

"Love you too, Bray," Bailey says.

"Love you too." says Mom.

Each of them glances at me as they say it.

I start to say another prayer in my head.

Thank you, Lord, for my family, MJ and Trey... in Jesus name, Amen.

Bible Scriptures used in Book

"This is the confidence we have in approaching God: that if we ask anything according to his will, he hears us."
1 John 5:14.

"Two is better than one because they have a good return for their labor. If either of them falls down, one can help the other up."
Ecclesiastes 4:9-10.

"The pain that you've been feeling can't compare to the joy that's coming."
Romans 8:18.

"With your right hand, you save me."
Psalm 138:7.

"Every good and perfect gift is from above, coming down from the Father of the heavenly lights, who does not change like shifting shadows."
James 1:17.

"So do not fear for I am with you; do not be dismayed for I am your God. I will strengthen you and help you. I will uphold you with my righteous hand."
Isaiah 41:10.

"Out of his fullness we have all received grace in place of grace already given."
John 1:16.
"We loved because he first loved us."
1 John 4:19.

"Carry each other's burdens, and in this way, you will fulfill the law of Christ."
Galatians 6:2

"We can rejoice too, when we run into problems and trials, for we know that they help us develop endurance. And endurance develops strength of character and character strengthens our confident hope of salvation And this hope will not lead to disappointment. For we know how dearly God loves us because he has given us the Holy Spirit to fill our hearts with his love."
Romans 3:5.

"He will cover you with his feathers, and under his wings you will find refuge; his faithfulness will be your shield and rampart."
Psalm 91:4.

"Jesus said to her, 'I am the resurrection and the life. The one who believes in me will live, even though they die; and whoever lives by believing in me will never die. Do you believe this?'"
John 11:25-26.

"Jesus went about all the cities and villages, teaching in their synagogues, and preaching the gospel of the kingdom, and healing every sickness and every disease among the people."
Mathew 9:35.

"For I know the plans I have for you," declares the LORD, 'plans to prosper you and not to harm you, plans to give you hope and a future.'"
Jeremiah 29:11.

"She is clothed with strength and dignity, and she laughs without fear of the future."
Proverbs 31:25

And the people all tried to touch him, because power was coming from him and healing them all.
Luke 6:19

…Next book. Coming soon.

His Closure

A Moment

Something you cherish or something you forget,
Sometimes it's the one thing you hope will last forever and
ever,

The feeling is either righteous or unbearable,
Leaving a mark in your life that'll never disappear,

You never want to let go,
So, you keep revisiting the moment to remember how good
it felt.

Sometimes the feeling is bad,
And maybe you should let go,

Or the thought of forgetting is worse,
So you choose to hold on to remember how you felt,

Hold on... hold on to the good moments,
Because feeling good, is one of the best feelings,

Braijene Fletcher

Mireya Chapter 1

"...because feeling good is one of the best feelings." I smile as I finish typing.

"Oh, one more thing..."

I start typing the P.S and press share when I'm done.

"Mireya, *vamos ahora.*" I hear my mom's voice from the hall.

"Coming, Mamá."

I push my chair into my small desk which is decorated with way too many leaf drawings and daisies, but I can't help it. I love nature. Nothing like reading a fantasy book or a book of poetry in the park. That is, if there was a "nice" public park I could walk to in my neighborhood. Unfortunately, *Mi familia y yo* live in Southwest Detroit. It's not the worst place on Earth but it has inconveniences. One of them being the fact that I can't sit under an oak tree and read a book without danger lurking! I stay in the house most of the time, but I go to *familia* parties where one happens every two weeks. I just would rather be by myself writing poetry in my room. It's cozy and "natury" looking. Especially because of the three, wide windows that face directly to my bed and I can see the dump of a backyard we have but at least the sun shines through. I grab my phone which has Frank O'Hara's quote from *'Having a Coke With You'* on the back of the case; along with brown leaves, brown roses, crinkled, brown paper. I almost forget my purse on the floor next to my desk as I scurry to my mirror hanging on the wall next to my bookshelf. I take a deep breath and scan my green tube dress, turning to the side.

Woah, okay, I'm graduating high school today. I hyperventilate a little.

Finally, I can leave that place.

I look at my hair to make sure the little ponytail in the back is tight enough. I run my fingers through the hair that's down in the back and take out two strands on either side to let hang. My makeup is done naturally -just how I like it- while my full lips are painted with a slight gold color. My coffin nails are matching with my gold heels. I thank God I went with mi amiga, Layla, to the mall the other day to get my nails done and to buy some products to care for my 3b hair.

I look so good.

I am snapped out of my thoughts when I get another call from Mamá. I walk out of my room, closing the door. I turn down the hall and walk into the living room to find my Abuela waiting for me. She sees me and smiles.

"Come give your Abuela a hug." she reaches her arms out.

I smile and hug her tightly.

"Estas preciosa." She cups my face.

"Gracias Abuela."

I can hear my mom yell from the kitchen. "Are you trying to be late for your own graduation, Reya?"

"Sorry," I whisper and move back from my grandmother as she starts coughing.

"Here's your water, Mamá." My mom gives Abuela her water and turns to face me. She gasps and starts to cry.

"You look beautiful, Reya." She rolls her tongue as she says my name.

"Thanks, Mamá." My laugh fades as grandmother starts coughing again.

"Are you okay, Abuela?" I kneel down to her.

"The nurse should be arriving soon," Mamá states.

"I will be fine. Now you go ahead and get your diploma, sí."

"*Sí*, Abuela." she smiles and I raise up.

"*¿Imágenes?*"

"Um, we'll take some pictures there. This place is not for it." I look at the raggedy, green sofa Abuela is sitting on with a small flat screen T.V Mamá was able to buy a few years ago…probably the only expensive thing in this house but everything functions. A small one-floor house with 3 bedrooms and the laundry room to separate my room from theirs. I come back to reality and watch as Mamá grabs the brush off the table and brushes her layered hair. The doorbell rings after a few seconds.

"*Esa es la enfermera.*" Mamá walks over to the door.

"Decided to straighten your hair, Mamá?"

Before opening the door, she says, "Just this once." Nurse Jackie walks in and they greet each other and Nurse Jackie congratulates me. I thank her and say goodbye to Abuela.

"See you there, Abuela." I walk out the door.

While driving in the car, I can tell Mamá is a bit worried about Abuela coming, but she insisted, and there's no arguing with Abuela.

"So how are you feeling? Nervous or anything?" Mamá asks.

"Not at all. I mean come on, I'm graduating today. These four years have gone by fast but I'm ready!" I look out the window.

"*Sí*...but you should be excited. The next step of your life is about to start." She smiles but I can tell there's another meaning behind her words.

"No, no, Mamá...I already know what you're thinking and I have my entire life for that."

"Okay but I got married when I was your age and everything was fine." I look at her and give her the 'really' face. She says, "Okay so maybe 'fine' isn't the word but we were strong for 27 years."

"That's because Antonio was the perfect boy. Well, man, I guess… but you told me mom always said to not rush those kinds of things."

"*Sí*, she believed that the perfect guy will come at the right time."

"Did he come at the right time for her?"

"He came and then left because he couldn't stay and then when he could again, it was too late. So I'd say, yes…he came at the perfect time because you're here, mija."

I smile to myself and stare out the window as we drive further away from our neighborhood.

*

"Okay, we're here."

I take in a breath as I see my peers walking into Chene Park. I unbuckle my seatbelt and unlock the door.

"Before you go, there's something I want to give you, Reya." Mom digs into her purse and pulls out a small box.

"This was your mother's necklace. She wanted me to give it to you the day you graduated."

I open the box and gush. "It's beautiful." I start to get teary-eyed.

"*Gracias*, Mamá." I pull her into a tight hug.

"You're welcome."

"Can you put it on me?" I giggle.

"Of course." She takes the necklace out and I turn my back towards her so she can put it on.

"Thank you."

We both get out of the car and I spot a limo pulling up before we cross the street. I keep my eyes locked on it as it comes to a stop. The door opens and a beautiful, olive skin girl with black curly hair gets out. She is wearing a pretty, black floral jumpsuit. Next is a lady who looks just like her but with blue eyes.

Genes are strong as heck.

As I'm about to look away, one of my peers with long, wavy blonde hair gets out with a tight, white dress. Lauren. The biggest wench in the school. She's not really a "wench" but that's what everyone calls her from the scandalous outfits she always wears. I mean her dress is the kind where only a thong can be worn with it. I mentally laugh and I watch her look cheery as she reaches her hand out to the door. After a few seconds a hand takes hers and climbs out is a familiar face.

Cameron Bates. The school's golden boy. I bite my lip as I take in his appearance.

He's wearing a light blue button-up shirt with a black jacket and pants to match. His dark, blondish hair is pushed up, making him look like some sort of model.

He smiles a bright smile as some of his friends come up to greet him. I wonder why he dates her. Or better, why does she date him? She's said numerous times that she doesn't date "white" boys when she's white herself... sounds like a personal thing.

"Woah seems like they have some money," Mom jokingly whispers in my ear, snapping me from my thoughts.

I smile at her as we continue to walk down the long path.

"Do you know them?" she asks.

"Yes. I have a class with the boy and the girl in the white dress." I give her a disgusted look and she laughs.

"Not a fan?"

I hear people running and I turn my head to the side of me to see Cameron with his girlfriend and his friends all talking and being loud.

"Definitely not," I whisper. "I don't think he likes me."

"Well, why not?"

"I don't know, it's just his vibe around me. Even though we've never actually spoken to each other."

"Hmm." Mom clings tighter on me and my eyes linger on the group of friends.

They stop walking and Cameron leans against a pole while clinging onto Lauren.

"Reya!" a voice shout from ahead of me.

I snap my head forward and look around to see where the voice came from.

"Layla!" I quickly walk up to her as she runs to me. We both crash into a big hug.

"Aw, you look so grown and beautiful."

"You look gorgeous," I smile.

Her hair, black and wavy. Her light pink dress and nails match her olive complexion.

"I know," She says, and we both laugh.

"We Mexicans gotta keep it tight." She acts like she does a little salsa and I shake my head at her with amusement.

"I am not Mexican," I say lowly.

"Yeah but everyone thinks so anyway."

"I'm gonna wait for your grandmother, Reya. She said she'll be here in a few minutes," Mom says.

"Okay," I say and she walks back to the parking lot.

"Wait…turn around," Layla instructs, and I do as she says. She gasps as my back faces her.

"Your butt looks too good in that!" she says way too loud, and I blush uncontrollably. I shush her and she laughs. I look over where Cameron is to see his whole group looking at me. One boy gets behind me to look at my bottom.

"I'd definitely hit that," he laughs and high fives one of his guys, while all except Cameron laugh.

"Bet you won't." I smile sarcastically and move a few feet away from them.

I hear his friends 'ooh' him as he tells them to shut up. I turn my head back and Cameron and I lock eyes for a split second. He has this stern look on his face before turning his attention back to his friends.

Weird.

*

Some time later

"Melissa Evans."

I wait anxiously for my name to be called next.

"Mireya Garcia." I stand up and walk up the stairs and onto the stage. I grab my diploma and shake the hands of my teachers and a few classmates. I throw my hands up and do a dance to the other side of the stage.

I graduated. Thank you, Jesus!

I walk down the stage and back to my seat. After the ceremony finishes, I make my way through the crowd to be greeted with another hug from Layla and one from her boyfriend who is also my boy-best friend. My feet hurt.

"Congratulations, Mireya." he smiles.

"Thanks, Antonio," I say with an accent.

"We're officially freshman in college...and you know what that means..." Layla smirks, "Legal drinking." She dances and makes me dance with her.

Layla's mom eventually finds us and makes us take at least 100 pictures together.

I didn't mind though, I want to savor this moment as much as possible.

"Okay, last one." Mrs. Martinez says.

Suddenly, I get a tap on my shoulder. I turn my head to see my Mamá and Abuela.

"I'm so proud of you, Reya." My Abuela pulls me into a tight hug.

"Thank you." I smile and give my Mamá a hug.

"Picture time," Mom says.

After taking a bunch of pictures once again, we make our way to the parking lot.

"See you at home, Abuela." I wave as she is escorted by the nurse.

Mom locks arms with me. "So, I was thinking of making your favorite flaky tacos for dinner."

"I was thinking I could make dinner."

"Oh okay." She smiles at me. "Mireya's cooking tonight, Mireya's cooking tonight."

I laugh as she starts to scurry closer to the sidewalk.

I get a tap on my shoulder.

"Hey, Mireya." His dark complexion is glowing in the sunlight.

"Hey, Joshua." I give him a hug. "Congratulations on getting valedictorian."

"Aw, thanks," he says while blushing, and I smile while looking away from him.

I scan forward as I see my mom at the curb.

"So I was thinking, now that we're out of school and it's summer…I was thinking we could…"

I keep my eyes locked forward. Worry takes over me as my mom steps out onto the street as a car is coming.

"Mom!" I scream out and start running to her.

She turns around in the middle of the road, without seeing the car. She notices my worried panic. I scream her name again. She looks to her right to see the car zooming straight towards her. She doesn't move out of the way quick enough. I stop in my tracks once I reach her.

"Mom?" I feel myself getting weaker and weaker as I approach her.

I can't control the tears running down my face. "Mom?"

I bend to her side as she lays there unconscious with blood on her face.

Cameron Chapter 1

In Bloomfield Hills, Michigan

"because feeling good is one of the best feelings." It reads. *"P.S...I'm graduating today so wish me luck."*

Hmm. I smile, shake my head with amusement, and type.

"I'm graduating too, *PWR_18.* Good luck with yours." I smirk and close my laptop.

"Cameron. Are you ready?" My mom peaks her head through my spacious room. I like my space. My own man cave.

"Yeah, Ma. Coming." I get off my bed and walk past my collection of short sleeve shirts as well as my pants on the bottom and then my leather outfits, and then my polo outfits, checkered shirts, Balenciaga fits, Louis Vuitton, and Nike fits. What can I say, I like clothes. I love that my closet looks like some store in the mall. I stop at the mirror to look at myself. I fix the sleeves of my Louis suit and run my fingers through my blonde hair finding a curled strand. I curse in my head.

This one's trying to curl again.

I take the little flat irons I left on purpose just in case this would happen and go over the strand that's curly.

"Perfect."

Let's get this over with.

I unplug the flat irons and walk out of my room to the grand staircase.

"There goes my dashing young boy." As I reach the last step, mom reaches her arms out and kisses my cheek.

"Mom, what century do you live in?" I whine and back away from her. "No mushy stuff."

She hits the back of my head, "I can get mushy as much as I want. You just look so handsome." She begins to cry.

Bipolar.

"Here we go." Cassie remarks as I'm just realizing her presence.

"Mom seriously, I'm only graduating."

"And that's a big success."

"Come on, mom. You spent 30 minutes on makeup. You wouldn't want to go to the graduation looking like Cassie, now would ya?"

Cassie scoffs, "You're a douche."

I roll my eyes as she consoles Mom and she sticks her tongue out at me. I stick my tongue back at her and she goes and gets Mom some tissues.

Suddenly the doorbell rings.

"Ooh, that's the photographer. Let's go." And just like that Mom is okay again. We walk out the door.

"Okay Cassie, you go first with Cam," Mom says, "I gotta fix myself real quick."

The photographer starts taking pictures.

"All you gotta do is mention a camera and Mom becomes Gigi Hadid," I laugh.

"More like Tyra Banks." Cassie looks up at me and smiles.

I give her a blank stare and clench my jaw.

"Woah, okay, I was just kidding, Cameron. You don't have to get so worked up." She rolls her eyes and gets inside the limo after bumping mom by mistake.

"What did you say?" Mom walks up to me and starts taking pictures.

"Nothing." I look sternly at the camera.

She lets out a frustrated sigh, "I just wish you didn't change yourself...you've been like this since you were fourteen, Cam. This isn't gonna change what happened-"

"I don't care, I'm not changing the way I feel or look." I walk away and get inside the limo, already wishing I can get back into bed...well, my future dorm bed.

*

By the time we reach Chene Park, I'm a bit agitated from the hour-long drive. Only because we had to pick up my girlfriend, Lauren from her mansion -not that I minded- but she talked non-stop about how she's gonna be the next Marilyn Monroe. Don't get me wrong, I KNOW she's gonna be the next Marilyn Monroe, but I can't stand when she starts mentioning that one actor from that big T.V show and started comparing me to him...It got better once I saw that Cassie was just as irritated as I was, and I took that as a chance to mess with her. I started asking Lauren about her fashion advice and how Cassie could do a lot better with her wardrobe. Cassie continued to give me death glares as Lauren criticized just about everything Cassie had on; respectfully but in a hilarious way. Once we pull up to the park, I look out and scan my classmates.

Sure won't be missing these suckers.

My mom excitedly opens the door and gets out following Cassie, Lauren, then me. I snake my arm around Lauren's hourglass figure and we start walking towards my friends.

*

"Just wait, Mireya Garcia will be mine," Jaxon states.

I honestly don't know why you like her.

"She is fine," Marcus swoons.

"Can we please stop talking about HER?" Lauren wines.

Cause I sure as heck don't wanna keep talking about her. I think to myself.

"You're just mad 'cause she's hotter than you," Marcus remarks, and my face instantly tightens.

"Sorry," he says and then, mumbles, "Even if it is true," but I still hear him.

I would put up a fight, but I could care less about that Mariah girl -or whatever her name is. And I'm planning to break up with Lauren anyway only because I don't want to have a girlfriend going into college, so might as well break it off at the beginning of summer.

"Oh, please, she don't have nothing on me," Lauren remarks.

I grab Lauren's hand as I now want to walk with my family but she pulls her hand away. I look back at her.

"Just give me a moment, Carol will be arriving soon. You can head in."

I tell her 'okay' and I turn to see my sister talking to that Mariah girl. They hug and the two friends leave.

"How do you know her?" I ask.

"Who? Mireya? I met her in ninth grade this year. Why? You think she's pretty?"

I shake my head, "Her and her friend were acting all ghetto a few minutes ago."

Cassie glares at me.

"Layla was hyping her friend up because she knows she looks good. It's what friends do."

"Yeah, maybe where they're from."

"I think you've forgotten where YOU'RE from." She rolls her eyes and begins to walk faster.

"Whatever," I huff.

I just want to graduate and be done with this place. I will no longer have to be around 'ghetto' people.

*

After the ceremony, my friends and family take a gazillion pictures in front of the park. I have my arm around Lauren's shoulder as we're all walking to my limo. Suddenly, a group of guys from the football team are driving out of control down the intersection to cross over to the parking lot. I spot a woman getting ready to cross. She stops walking and I turn my head away for a second before hearing a crash sound and seeing that Mariah girl in the street with the woman lying in her lap…well dang…sucks to be them.